W9-BZD-038

Visual Supports
for People with Autism

A Guide for Parents and Professionals

Marlene J. Cohen, Ed.D., BCi
Donna L. Sloan, M.A., BCBA

Woodbine House ◊ 2007

Library of Congress Cataloging-in-Publication Data

Cohen, Marlene J.
  Visual supports for people with autism : a guide for parents and professionals / Marlene J. Cohen and Donna L. Sloan. -- 1st ed.
     p. cm. -- (Topics in autism)
  Includes bibliographical references and index.
  ISBN-13: 978-1-890627-47-8
  ISBN-10: 1-890627-47-X
  1. Autistic children--Education. 2. Learning disabled--Education. 3. Visual aids. I. Sloan, Donna L. II. Title.
  LC4717.C64 2007
  371.94--dc22

                                                                    2006102017

Manufactured in the United States of America

First edition

10   9   8   7   6   5   4   3   2   1

In memory of my cousin Billy,
who provided me with my first exposure to autism.
I had no knowledge of autism at the time,
but I believe you touched my life in a way
that guided the decision to devote my career
to helping people with this diagnosis.
M.C.

In memory of my parents,
Laverne & Ralph A. Vicidomini, Sr.,
my first and very best teachers.
D.S.

Table of Contents

Acknowledgements

After many years of experience in the classroom as teachers, trainers, and supervisors, we have seen the power of visual strategies for learners with autism spectrum disorders. We have met and worked with many creative educators and families who also used visual strategies to support their children and students. The strategies shown throughout this book are a small collection of the hundreds we have seen and used. We hope this book serves as an inspiration to you to be creative and incorporate visual supports into your teaching.

Thank you to Dr. Mel Levine for allowing us to use his body of work as the framework for this publication. Your work illuminating the learning process has motivated us to understand some of the specific learning strengths and challenges of people with ASD and to use this information to raise some of the ceilings previously thought to exist.

We are thankful to work in a supportive environment with our colleagues at the Douglass Developmental Disabilities Center, including: Maria Arnold, Marlene Brown, Lara Delmolino, Rita Gordon, Barbara Kristoff, Robert La Rue, Mary Jane Weiss, and especially Jan Handleman and Sandra Harris. We would also like to thank the staff who shared some strategies that they have used with their learners, especially Lisa Stinemeyer and Jen Woods. We appreciate those who have allowed us to use their image in some of the examples: Aylin Rollano-Moreno, Ian Bober, Pamela Lubbers, Mary Sens-Azara, Tanya Lindley, Stacay Williams, Maria Grace Pardee, Faith Torres, Dania Matthews, Cathy Avasso, Melissa McCulloch, Nicole Winston, Jacqui Abrams, Mark Bannon, Sean Neenan, Enzo and Sophia Zoroni (Adam), Bobbie and Bill Gallagher (Alanna), Carolyn Calix (Christian), Michelle Falco (David), Frank and Stephanie Basile (Joey), Bob and Cindy LaRue (Alexandra), Allan and Sharon Kiil (Kaitlyn and Jeremy). We are particularly grateful to the many students we have worked with and their families who have taught us to keep looking for answers to problems we were previously unable to solve. Thanks for your patience and insight!

Marlene would like to thank Marty, her husband of twenty-five years, and her three children, Dan, Kyle, and Chelsea, for their undying love and support, as well as their tolerance of many long work hours and periodically worn temperament. You bring meaning and inspiration to my life. She would also like to send her appreciation to two very close friends, Sandi Sersen and Peter Gerhardt, who somehow always believed she could complete this book. Thanks for your faith in me.

Donna would like to thank her husband, Ken, for his unconditional love, support, and encouragement. Thanks to her brothers, Ralph Jr. and Michael, who have given lots of brotherly love and advice, and to Sharon, who is like a sister to her. A special note of appreciation goes to Ralph III, Steven, and Amy, who bring so much joy to her life.

Foreword

The field of teaching students with autism spectrum disorders is rapidly advancing, and professionals and families are being provided with a greater number of teaching tools. For example, we now know that these students have individual instructional needs, and that "one size fits all" does not apply when selecting teaching strategies. This appreciation for individual differences and the need for a range of methods is particularly found in the field of Applied Behavior Analysis (ABA). In the last decade, ABA methods have expanded beyond the traditional use of discrete trial instruction, to include a wide range of strategies and different ways to approach language and social skills development. One area of particular interest has been the use of visual supports in teaching.

In *Visual Supports for People with Autism,* Marlene Cohen and Donna Sloan provide parents and professionals with a highly useful resource for strategically and systematically using visual supports to teach students with autism spectrum disorders. Through the use of case studies, the book helps the reader to assess the learning styles of students and to decide when, and for which learning challenges, visual supports can be useful. The authors have organized the book according to specific learning and behavioral issues, to help the reader quickly find information that can be useful for a particular student.

Marlene Cohen and Donna Sloan have drawn upon their many years of experience in working with students with autism spectrum disorders to create a highly practical guide for parents and professionals. The use of this book will greatly simplify the process of determining when and how to use visual supports. *Visual Supports for People with Autism* will be a valuable addition to any personal or professional collection.

Jan S. Handleman, Professor & Director
Douglass Developmental Disabilities Center
Rutgers, The State University
New Brunswick, New Jersey

Introduction

People with autism spectrum disorders have learning strengths and weaknesses. For many, auditory input, such as speech, is one of the most challenging modalities, while information absorbed through sight may be much more easily mastered. The goal of this book is to help you draw on your child's strengths to support areas of weakness. Although not all children with autism are stronger visual than auditory learners, many are. This book will help you in teaching your child if he or she processes visual cues more readily than auditory cues.

If you are unsure whether your child is a visual learner, try these strategies:

- **Observe your child's responses to information presented verbally or visually.** If your child has a tendency to learn more quickly when visual cues such as pictures, photos, or objects are presented than if information is presented using verbal input alone, then your child may be a visual learner.
- **Ask others working with your child for input about how they think your child learns best.** For example, ask, "Does my child perform better for picture identification than for when responding to spoken one-step commands?"
- **Try presenting information using verbal input alone versus verbal and visual input and see how your child responds.** For example, does your child respond more consistently to "Get your coat" when you use a visual cue (point to coat location) than when you don't use the cue? Temple Grandin, an adult with autism, speaks about her need to translate verbal language into pictures in order for her to develop an understanding of the concept(s) being presented. You can make this process easier for your child by providing the visual cues from the start.

Perhaps your child appears to understand everything you say and responds accordingly. Students with a diagnosis of Asperger's syndrome may have strong verbal skills and may not require extensive use of visual cues. It is a known fact, however, that information presented both auditorially and visually is more likely to be remembered (Sousa 2001). If we add active participation, or kinesthetic input, we increase recall even further. So, even though your child may not be a visual learner, he or she may still benefit from some of the strategies explored in this book.

Do you need to create visual supports for everything being taught? The answer is no. You should select visual supports for concepts that have been difficult for your child to learn. Try out a support that you feel will be helpful and then determine whether it increases your child's ability to learn the concept. Once you have done this successfully for several skills, you will establish the best type of visual support for your child.

Both parents and teachers can use visual strategies to help a child learn. This book is best used as a reference. You need not read every chapter. Instead, select chapters to read based on the specific learning challenge that your child is encountering. Chapter 10 describes the success of a student whose response to visual supports made a significant difference in his learning outcomes as well as his placement in a less restrictive environment. Although not every child responds this well to the addition of visual supports, it is helpful to see how they helped this particular child as you are considering the needs of your own.

Chapters 3 to 8 focus on specific areas of learning that may be of concern for children with autism spectrum disorders. These areas include:

1. **Difficulty with language,** including the inability to learn language labels (expressively or receptively); verbal language that appears garbled and out of order; inconsistent responding to verbal instructions; and speech development that is behind the chronological age of your child. If this describes your child, you can refer to Chapter 3 of this book.

2. **Difficulty with memory,** including being able to respond accurately on one day, but not necessarily on another; inability to remember the location of items despite repeated presentations; difficulty remembering instructions; and having special difficulty with memory when the response requires performance of a skill in a different location. Chapter 4 provides more detail about deficits in this area of learning as well as some possible solutions.

3. **Temporal/sequential skill deficits,** which may be exhibited by: the ability to follow a single-step direction, but the inability to follow multiple step directions; inability to relate an experience in sequential order (first, I ___, then I ___, etc.); a tendency to be late; the inability to plan enough time to complete a project; and the inability to sequence pictures. You can go to Chapter 5 for further discussion of problems in this area.

4. **Difficulty with attending,** which may be exhibited through inconsistent performance (performs accurately at one point and inaccurately

at another); a low tolerance for long periods of work, particularly if the task is difficult (low level of mental effort); impulsive rule-breaking; is easily distracted; difficulty with short-term memory (ability to process information thoroughly enough to use it; and over- or under-attention to detail. Attention deficits are discussed in greater detail in Chapter 6.

5. **Lack of motivation,** which can be demonstrated through the inability to follow through with a task or skill that the child has mastered; neglecting to complete tasks or chores; and lack of interest in learning new skills (which may be noticed after a pattern of failed academic experiences). Chapter 7 covers ideas for increasing motivation using visual supports.

6. **Social skills deficits** are overwhelmingly noticeable in learners with autism. Examples of social skills deficits include the inability to make and keep friends; showing an interest in joining peers, but being unable to determine the skills necessary to join in; lack of empathy as demonstrated by comments that are insensitive to the feelings of others; lack of awareness of what behaviors are perceived as socially appropriate or socially inappropriate; and inability to pick up on social rules and conventions. The area of social skills deficits is illustrated with greater detail in Chapter 8.

General Guidelines for Selecting Visual Supports

- The area of deficit (e.g., memory, language, attention) may not be perfectly clear at first.
- Trial and error will help you to decide which strategies yield the most success.
- Use your data to determine effectiveness of a support (pre and post data), as discussed in Chapter 1.
- Don't hesitate to try a visual support because you don't know whether it will yield the results you are looking for. No one has ever been hurt by implementing a short trial of a new support.
- If a support is not working after two weeks, discontinue it so as not to develop over-reliance on an unnecessary support.

Visual supports include a wide variety of cues that can enable any person to perform skills with greater independence. We all use visual supports in some aspect of our lives. We use a calendar as a means of remembering appointments and scheduled activities. We might highlight important parts of a text when taking a class. Post-It® notes are widely used to communicate messages or to help us recall thoughts that might otherwise be forgotten. Diagrams accompany items that require assembly. It is important to recognize that we can develop our own strategies to accommodate for weaknesses we may have in the learning process. Once we realize this, we now envision how we can incorporate a wide range of supports for people with autism who may not be able to communicate areas of difficulty.

Types of visual supports for children with autism spectrum disorders can include, but are not limited to:

- pictures/photos/words as a system of communication, scheduling system, or a cuing system for skill performance;
- the use of conceptual maps or graphic organizers for concept development, development of conversational skills and language expansion, or for recall;
- the use of motivational systems for teaching delayed gratification or as a cue to increase the student's motivation; and
- the introduction of Social Stories or other social skills cuing methods to increase social competence.

In order to select an appropriate support, you must have a basic understanding of the many components of the learning process (e.g., understanding and use of language, short-term and long-term memory, temporal/sequential skills, attending skills, motivation, and social skills). We are using information from Dr. Mel Levine's books *Educational Care* (1994), *A Mind at a Time* (2002), and *The Myth of Laziness* (2003) as the basis for understanding this process. Dr. Levine is a professor of pediatrics at the University of North Carolina Medical School and director of its Clinical Center for the Study of Development and Learning. He has had many years of experience working with students who demonstrate a wide variety of learning disabilities. Although his research is not specific to autism, we believe that people with autism have additional challenges not specific to their primary disability which may have a negative impact on learning. We are using Dr. Levine's framework for the learning process in order to assess the learning challenges of people with autism.

In addition, we have used some of the research contained in the book *How the Brain Learns* (Sousa, 2001) to further understand the conditions for optimal and sub-optimal learning. The particular emphasis in this book is David Sousa's understanding of how the memory process works.

Part of the art of using visual supports is knowing when to "fade" (gradually withdraw) them, as well as when to use them. Consequently, in Chapter 9, we address how to fade visual supports. The chapter provides a variety of strategies for visual support fading, which can be used for the supports that you develop using ideas from Chapters 3 to 8. This will allow you to design a fading format that best meets the needs of the student you are teaching. Chapter 9 also addresses the question of whether or not supports need to be faded.

The book concludes with the story of a student who far surpassed initial expectations as a result of implementing a variety of visual supports—which provides a lesson on how to avoid imposing arbitrary ceilings on the performance of a person with autism. Our educational motto is "Safe, respected, and competent." We believe that when students feel that nothing bad will happen in the educational environment, and that the educators respect their dignity and need for independence and believe that they *can* perform in an educational setting, anything can happen.

The Features of a Good Visual Support

Every child's needs are unique. Keeping this in mind, it is important that each visual support is individualized to meet his or her skill level, age, and interest. The purpose of this book is to provide you with a foundation of ideas to help you in creating your own visual supports. As discussed below, there are some general guidelines that you should keep in mind.

Tailoring Visual Supports to the User's Needs

Before you invest the time and effort to create a visual support for a particular student, you should have an idea of what features will be most helpful for him. If you do not know him well, you may need to take some time to determine how he responds best to different types of pictures, colors, size, and other variables.

When the student is initially learning to use a particular support, you should begin with one to two supports at a time and systematically increase to the desired number. For example, if you are using a picture schedule to increase independent play, start with one picture. When the child is able to respond independently to one picture, add another until he can complete both activities independently. Continue to add one picture at a time, until the child is able to complete as many activities as is appropriate for his age. You may want to watch some typically developing same-age peers to estimate your end goal.

Type of Photos or Pictures

The selection of photos or drawn/commercially created pictures is another consideration. Depending on the student's age or cognitive abilities, he may respond best to:

- objects that represent the item,
- photographs,
- life-like drawings, or
- symbolic drawings (such as the Picture Communication Symbols©).

You should expose your student to each option to see which one he responds to best. Some students with autism spectrum disorders have difficulty responding to photographs or pictures. Pictures and photos are symbols of the items they represent, and the person you are working with may not be able to respond to symbols at

this time. Instead, he may respond to the use of small objects that represent the actual item. Dollhouse accessories or craft supplies are good sources of these objects. Some speech and language catalogs might also offer objects you could use, but are usually more expensive. If it is possible that your student might place these small objects in his mouth, you will need to secure them to a flat surface that is too large to swallow or put them in a clear container.

If the student is able to identify both photographs and pictures, present both options separately to see which one he responds to more consistently and accurately. If there seems to be no difference in response, look at other variables such as the student's interest in pictures versus photos. Does he hold on to one longer? Does he sustain eye contact with you longer when you are using one vs. the other? If you know the individual well, you will be the best judge of how he responds to something he likes or doesn't like. If you don't know him well, seek feedback from those who do.

This book will present a variety of other supports in addition to pictures, photos, and objects. You may be curious as to why one is selected versus another. As a general rule, pictures/photos/miniature objects should be used to represent the actual object or the activity associated with that object. The use of color can help cue the individual to orient to a particular position (e.g., the start button on a dryer or the play button on a CD player). Color can also be used to indicate order (e.g., red = subject and blue = verb in sentence development) or to highlight the key idea (e.g., key words in a set of written instructions such as a recipe). The colors of green, yellow, and red are often used to indicate start, slow down, and finished.

It will be important to establish whether the child you are working with is colorblind. The following web site could be useful in assessing someone for this problem: http://members.shaw.ca/hidden-talents/vision/color/colorblind2.html. Typically, the individual would need to have some identification skills in order for the test to be valid. If there is any question of whether your child is color blind, use black and white photos as your starting point.

Other types of visual supports include (but are not limited to) numbers to indicate order, icons to indicate what the individual should attend to, and size to indicate hierarchical order. This book is not intended to list all of the possible options that could be used. Be creative and try out some of your own ideas!

Durability

Younger children (and some older ones too) can be rough with materials, so durability is a consideration. Learning to make supports durable enough may require some trial and error on your part, but some general principles are to select materials that last after being bent or that are safe when thrown. A lamination machine is an excellent investment and can be used to make pictures, flash cards, or other paper material waterproof and less resistant to tearing. If you do not wish to purchase a laminating machine, clear Contact paper will work, but requires more cutting and is a little more difficult to use. (It is sticky and can tear materials if moved during the covering process.) Some office supply stores can laminate visual supports for you, but this option is typically more costly.

If the support is not going to receive a lot of wear and tear, poster paper, foam board, or corrugated cardboard might be good options. They can be purchased at a local office supplies store. A quick trip to a local store can usually help you assess the advantages and disadvantages of a particular material.

Portability

When creating visual supports, it is a good idea to determine if they will be stationary or portable. Typically, it is easier for young children and children who have weak fine motor skill development to manipulate larger supports. In some cases, the need to have a larger support may dictate the need for it to stay in one place. Smaller visual supports may be in order if a student with ASD is included in a regular education classroom. In this case, it will be especially important to take into account whether the support draws undue attention to the student's differences. This should be a consideration regardless of the child's placement, but it is particularly critical in social situations with typically developing children.

If the supports will move with the child, you will have to consider the child's size. If he is small or less inclined to exert physical effort, his supports should be as lightweight as possible. You will also have to consider how the supports will travel. The support can be fashioned with a handle or can be placed in some type of carrier such as a fanny pack, small backpack, small box with a handle, or similar item, or it can be clipped to a belt or belt loop.

In a day and age where many of us are carrying multiple personal items (cell phones, pagers, PDAs, etc.), there are a variety of options that could be considered. If you plan to place the visual support in a carrying case, you will want to find the case before creating the support so you can ensure that it will fit. You will also have to think about how to keep the support in one piece while in the carrying case, so the student does not become frustrated and confused the next time he needs to use it.

Clarity

In order to develop a visual support that is effective, you will want to test it for clarity. Develop a test sample and try it out with your child. Is the support salient (obvious) enough for the child to respond in the manner expected? For example, if you are using a colored background as a cue for correct responding, is it obvious enough for the child to cue into? Use colors that are unusual and bright so they attract attention. Office supply stores have aisles that are filled with a wide selection of markers, so have fun selecting colors that will be sure to attract your child's attention.

If you are using pictures or photos, are they clear and crisp? If you need to enlarge a picture or photo, sometimes the result can be grainy and less clear. Clarity is particularly important if the visuals will be kept at a distance. Size here will also be important. Larger visuals are needed for longer distances.

If the visual support is meant to represent a single item or concept, make sure that this is the only concept represented in the photo. For example, if you are using a photo of a door, don't include the whole house in the photo. Some students with autism may be over-selective and may cue into other aspects of the visual support than the aspect that you are teaching.

You may be using a visual support that indicates that the student needs to respond with an action. Is that response obvious or would there be a clearer way the response can be represented? There will be times when you encounter a concept that cannot be represented as clearly as you would like. If this is the case, you will have to teach the response first before using it as a cue.

Age Appropriateness

Age appropriateness becomes a concern when the student is about eight years of age. Age appropriateness is an important consideration because we do not wish to convey the message that people with ASD are young children in larger bodies. Appearance becomes more important to typical children as they get into the middle childhood ages. Students with ASD are more likely to be accepted if they use items that are appropriate for their age. For example, many cartoons (with some exceptions) are appropriate only for younger students.

So, how do you determine if a support is age appropriate? The best way is to spend some time observing typically developing peers. Could you imagine one of those children carrying/using this visual support? You might also want to speak with some of them to get a feel for what would be accepted and what would not. Neighborhood children who you know and trust are often a good option.

Response Effort Required

As with all students, some students with ASD do not like to exert a tremendous amount of energy. Consequently, you should look at how easy it would be to use the support you are designing. If a child has poor fine motor skills and the support requires the use of a fine pincer grasp, he is more likely to resist using it than if it were easier to manipulate.

Visual supports should be designed to make life easier. If they require the student to make a good deal of extra effort, your visual cues may actually lead to problematic behavior. It is easier and more efficient if you take your child's motor skill development, endurance, and behavior tendencies into mind before developing the supports. For example, if your child has a tendency to throw items, secure the photos or pictures with Velcro to make this less likely. Also, limit the number of items you present at any given time, reducing the likelihood that the supports will be knocked off the table or work area. Your goal should be to make life easier and more understandable for your student. You'll get there faster if the response effort is reasonable and reinforcement is likely to occur when the student uses the visual support (e.g., he feels pleased with himself when he completes a task successfully, is praised by the teacher, or receives some kind of concrete reward). That is, he is either reinforced by the natural consequences or by an adult.

Possible Materials Needed

Most of the visual supports described in later chapters can be constructed with the following materials:

- Scissors
- Colored paper
- Velcro
- Laminating or clear Contact paper
- Camera (preferably digital)
- Colored markers
- Clip art
- Binders
- Poster board
- Foam board
- Bulletin board
- Dry erase board
- Dry erase markers
- Index cards
- Plastic sheet protectors
- Miniature common objects
- Glue stick or spray adhesive
- Manila folders (plain or colored)
- Labels
- Stickers
- Picture books
- Magazines
- Magnets
- Clipboards
- Calendar
- Highlighters
- Post-It™ flags

- Photo albums
- Wallets
- Loose leaf rings
- Timer
- Storage bins

Determining the Effectiveness of a Visual Support

While the authors of this book are Behavior Analysts, determining the effectiveness of a visual support does not have to involve the collection of additional data, extensive charting, or comprehensive assessment. A good educational program should have some form of objective measurement already in place. You can easily track a change in progress by marking that point on the date the visual support was introduced and by comparing progress before and after the introduction of that support. What you want to see is an increase in accuracy, rate of responding, and/or more rapid skill acquisition.

For example, if you are using accuracy measures, you want to look at the trend or direction of the data before and after the introduction of a visual support. A good way to do this would be to evaluate any differences between the data three to five days before implementation and the three to five days after implementation. The next page shows some examples of progress, no change, and regression.

If you are monitoring progress by rate of responding, you can compare the average rate per minute of each skill (how many can be done in a one-minute timeframe) to the average rate per minute after the implementation of a visual support. As an example, your student may be able to add an average of two equations in one minute before a visual support was used and add an average of six equations per minute after. In other word, the student can add problems more quickly with the use of a visual support.

Difficult tasks can often cause an increase in problematic behavior. You can also measure the success of a visual support by tracking the frequency of problematic behavior both before and after you initiate the strategy. If problematic behavior decreases or is eliminated, then you know you have succeeded in making the task easier for your child to perform.

Whatever measure you use, make sure you are being objective in your assessment of progress. It is often easy to think we are making a difference when we are not, or to think we are having no effect when we are. When a support is successful, you will want to expand its use to other areas where the student is having difficulty. If you don't experience success, you may want to modify your strategy or try something new. Multiple failures may mean that visual supports are not a helpful strategy for this particular student.

Good Progress

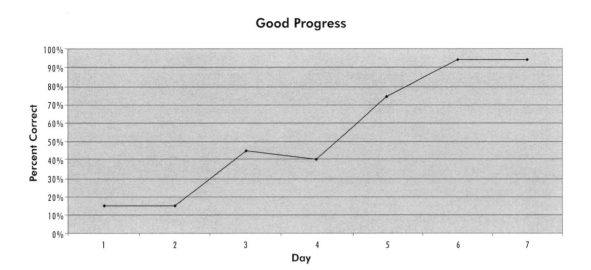

No Progress

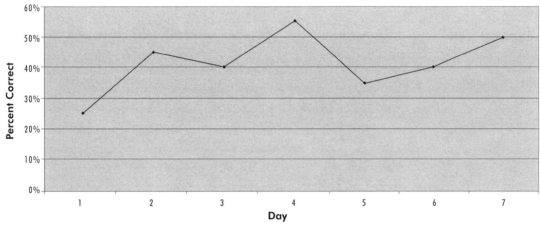

Regression

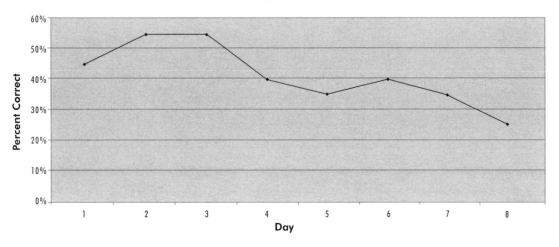

Some Commonly Used Visual Supports

A Primer

While this book was developed as a result of the personal experiences of the authors, the use of visual supports with persons with ASD is not new. Some of the supports frequently referenced in this book have been helping students for over ten years. We have listed below, in alphabetical order, the types we discuss the most often, along with a brief description. If you wish to obtain more detailed information, please refer to our list of references for this information.

◼ Activity Schedules

Activity schedules can help a child with ASD learn to perform a sequence or a set of activities with greater independence. Technically speaking, an activity schedule is "a set of pictures or words that cues someone to engage in a sequence of activities" (McClannahan & Krantz, 1999). Pictures or photographs are often inserted into page protectors with one or two per page and placed into binders (see Figure 7.10, for example). The child is then taught to refer to the pictures in order and to do the activity that is cued. For example, pictures of a puzzle, a magnetic toy, and a container of yogurt may cue the child to first go to the shelf where her toys are kept, get down the puzzle, and put it together; then retrieve her magnetic toy to play with; and finally, approach her mother to request a snack. At first, the child may need various types of prompts to follow the activity schedule, but eventually, she learns to follow her schedule on her own.

An excellent resource for the implementation of a picture schedule is Lynn McClannahan and Patricia Krantz's *Activity Schedules for Children with Autism*

(1999) published by Woodbine House. The book teaches the reader the skills necessary to use a picture schedule (understanding of what a picture represents) and a systematic way of introducing schedules, one item at a time, until the desired result is obtained. Suggestions for helping the child progress to using written words in place of pictures are also included.

Whether you use *Activity Schedules for Children with Autism* or decide to try introducing picture sequences on your own, the use of visuals can help to build independence. Many parents have successfully used picture sequences to structure independent play for their son or daughter. In school, teachers can use pictures to indicate the schedule of the day, or a particular set of activities they wish the student to complete independently. Start with one picture and slowly build to several. Keep in mind what typically developing peers might be expected to do as a guideline. Children with autism need a balance of independent and social activities.

Calendars

There are many types of calendars readily available to teachers and parents that can be used as visual supports. Some are large and represent an entire month. They can be found in dry erase format. Here the day/date/month are written into the correct position by hand and then adjusted for the following month. Calendars with pre-printed day/date/month are also available. The dates are usually attached by Velcro or magnet and can be rearranged monthly. These larger calendars are good for indicating important events or holidays and can provide the individual with a sense of the time that will elapse before a certain event will occur. For example, an adult with ASD who had difficulty handling the absence of a favorite staff member used a calendar to mark off the days that passed before he returned from paternity leave. In the past, the adult had found it very frustrating to deal with this type of situation due to his uncertainty about when the person would return.

Calendars that provide spaces for listing activities by time of day can also be very useful. They can be found formatted one day at a time or one week at a time. This type of calendar can be used to represent a series of activities that are scheduled to occur during a day. In general, this kind of calendar is best suited for older children and adults with some reading skills. You will need to put some thought into considering how much information a particular individual can process at a time. It is best to keep a calendar simple and to gradually increase the amount of information presented at one time.

After a student can use a calendar that has been filled out by a teacher or parent, you may succeed in instructing her to write her own schedule on a calendar if she has the reading and writing skills to do so. Being able to independently write a daily schedule is a skill that can be very useful in adult life.

Checklists

Checklists are good supports for helping a student remember a sequence of behaviors, items that need to be purchased in a grocery story, or a "to do" list of chores. Primarily designed for students who are older and who read, they provide visual representation of the parts of an activity that have been completed versus the ones that have not. For example, you might use a checklist of steps involved in using a copier:

1. Orient the paper as shown in sheet feeder.____
2. Place page(s) in sheet feeder. ____
3. Set number of copies needed. ____
4. Set format (collated or stapled).____
5. Press start. ____
6. Retrieve copies. ____
7. Press clear to remove settings for next user. ____

A student who reads well but has a tendency to forget how to perform multiple-step tasks can check off each step until the entire list is completed. Eventually, students who are strong visual learners rely less and less on the list because the visual representation of the checklist is stored into memory.

At home, a child could use a checklist to remember the chores she needs to do. In this case, it may not matter what order the list is completed as long as all of the items have been accomplished. That list might look something like this:

____ Feed the cat
____ Take out garbage
____ Do homework
____ Brush teeth

The items can be checked off in order of the child's preference, allowing for a greater sense of control over her environment. You could also create a checklist using pictures.

Color Coding

We use color coding in our everyday life. For example, we all know that a green traffic light signals a driver to go and a red light signals stop. At work, we may color code our file folders so that the red folders represent personal information, the blue folders represent work material, and the yellow represent information that needs to go to someone else. Public school teachers often ask students to color code a subject area to make it easier to find content-related information. The science teacher may want students to bring in a blue binder and blue pocket folders for science class.

The purpose of color coding is to either highlight an important feature (e.g., red ink to indicate corrections that need to be made) or to represent a category, as in the science example above. Highlighters, markers, colored pencils, and colored background are all examples of some of the tools you might use to color code instructional material. There are a variety of examples in this book for you to choose from or you could create your own ideas to meet the needs and interests of your child.

Comic Strip Conversations

This visual support was developed by Carol Gray (1994). It is best described as a positive behavior support, meaning the focus is placed on instruction and re-inforcement of the desired behavior rather than punishment of the undesired be-havior. Carol Gray developed this tool to address the needs of young students who have more difficulty with oral and written language. The comic strip conversation incorporates simple cartoon figures and symbols into a comic strip format (a se-quence of related pictures). For example, if a child is having trouble sharing arts and crafts materials at school, a comic strip conversation might be created with cartoon panels that show: 1) one student asking another student to pass the scis-sors, 2) the second student responding appropriately if she is not yet done with the scissors, and 3) the first student thanking her for passing the scissors.

According to research (Rogers & Myles 2001, Rowe 1999), this visual support can reduce challenging behavior of students with ASD who have below average verbal ability. Comic Strip Conversations may not be appropriate for students who have not yet mastered the concept of sequencing, as a comic strip relates a sequence of verbal responses between the communicator and the listener.

See Figures 3.19 and 8.13 in the color insert for examples of Comic Strip Conversations.

Graphic Organizers

Graphic organizers are used to organize information or thoughts in such a way that a visual learner would be more likely to comprehend and recall the information. They can be simple and contain only a few ideas, or complex enough to visually represent more complicated concepts such as are taught in a biology lesson.

If you are good at using the Internet to gather information and resources, you will find that many educators generously offer their examples for use by other teachers and parents. Using your computer's search engine, enter "graphic orga-nizers." You will find a multitude of examples and styles of organizers.

On pages 13-17 we have included several graphic organizers that can be adapted for use by students of different ages and capabilities. They include:

- Figure 2.1—About Me: An organizer that can be used to help children gain a better understanding of themselves or to introduce themselves to others; can be adapted for nonreaders by allowing them to draw or paste pictures of activities.
- Figure 2.2—Word Web: An organizer that encourages children to ex-pand their knowledge about a concept or new vocabulary word.
- Figure 2.3—Star: Best used to brainstorm ideas or to illustrate multiple characteristics of a particular topic.
- Figure 2.4—Flow Chart: Best used to show a sequence of instructions for a multi-step process or to show hierarchical relationships such as a family tree.

Fig. 2.1—Person Graphic Organizer

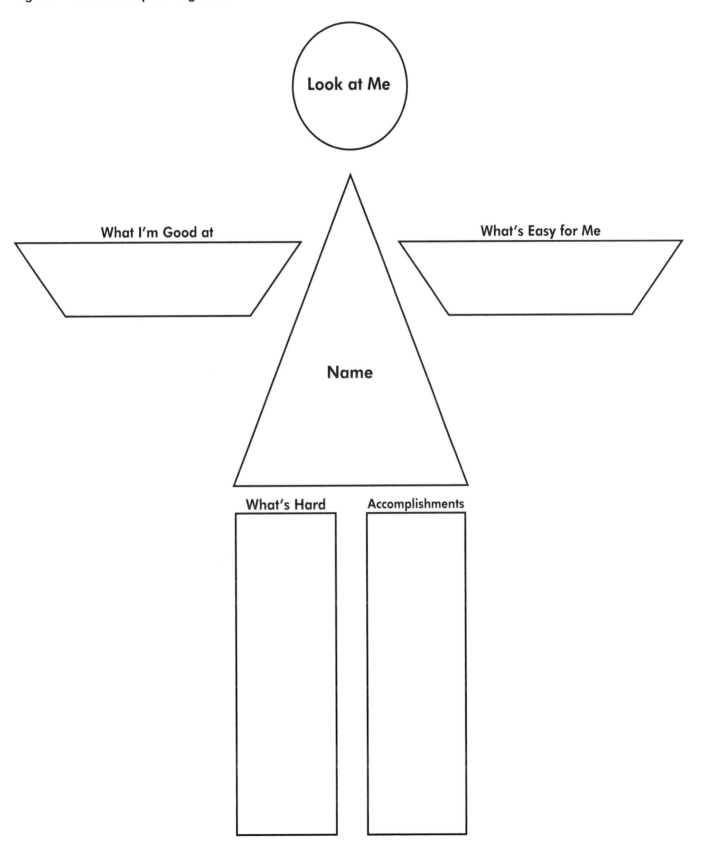

Fig. 2.2—Cluster/Word Web
Write your topic in the center and the details in the smaller circles.

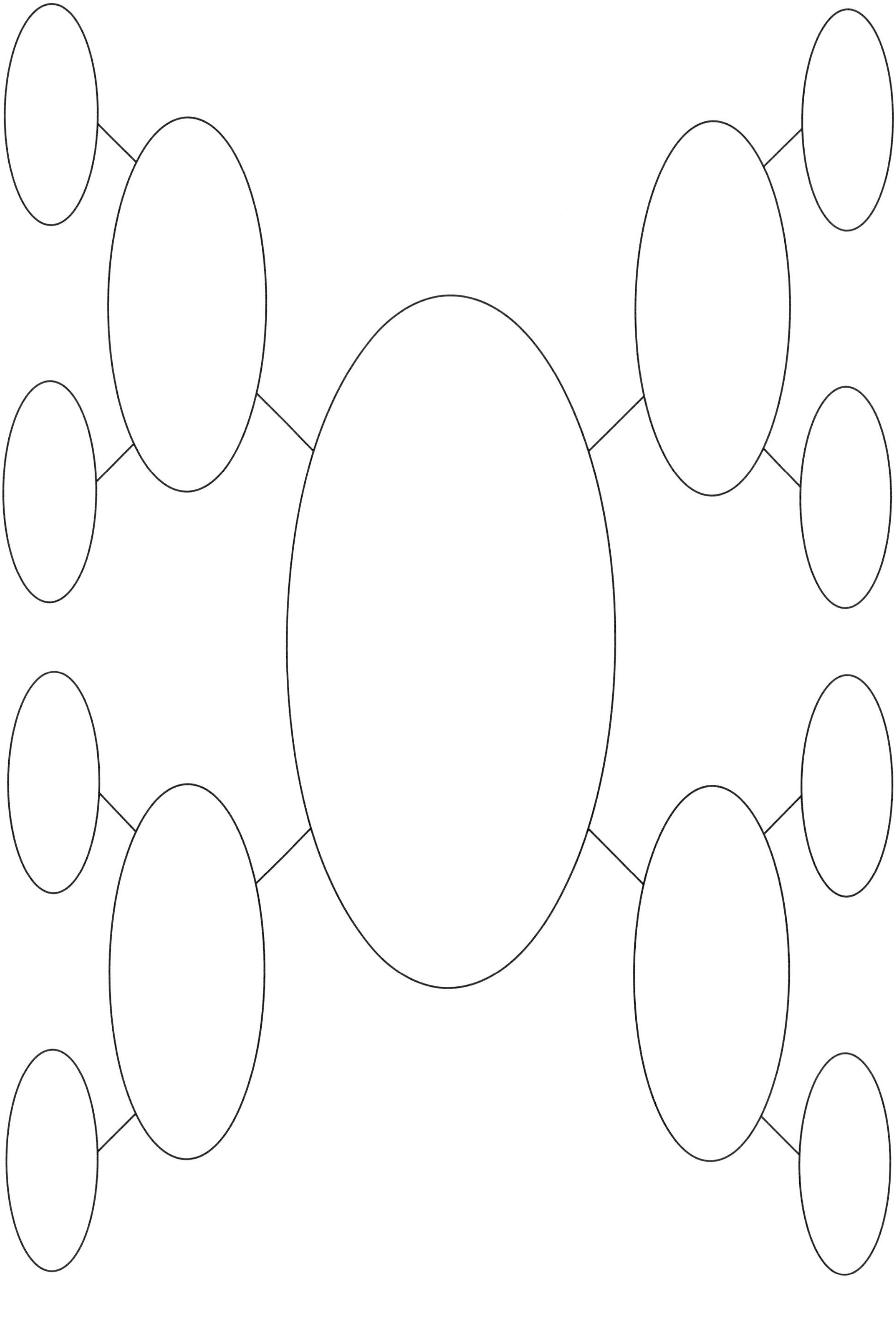

Fig. 2.3—Star Graphic Organizer

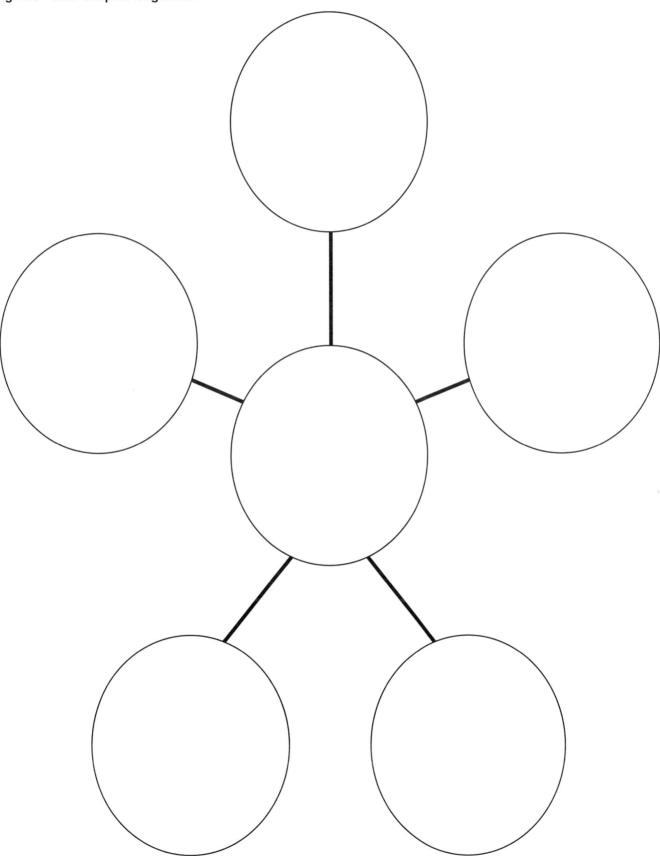

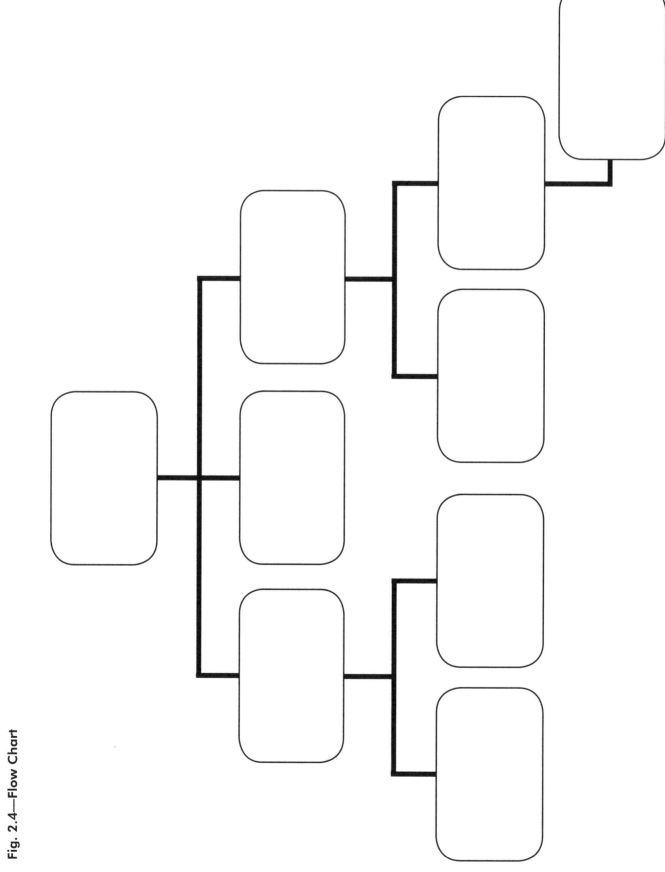

Fig. 2.4—Flow Chart

Fig. 2.5—Cycle Graphic Organizer

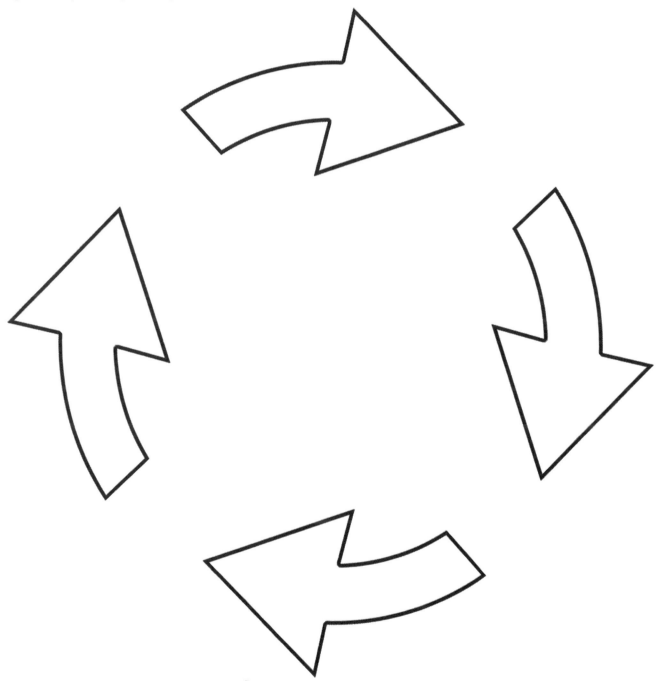

- Figure 2.5—Cycle: Displays how items are related to each other, when the cycle will be repeated (e.g., the life cycle of a butterfly).

When teaching a student with ASD to use a graphic organizer for the first time, you will need to complete the entire organizer, including text. As the student becomes more familiar with the use of graphic organizers, you can begin to fade your assistance—by filling in only some of the text and letting the student complete the parts she can. Eventually, allow the student to complete all of the text. An advanced learner could make her own graphic organizer in its entirety.

Take a look at our reference list at the back of the book for some good sources of graphic organizers. You are bound to come up with at least one good idea for organizing information in a visual format.

Manipulatives

The use of manipulatives has been incorporated into early education for many years. I can still remember my kids counting bundles of ten popsicle sticks until ten sets of ten signaled "100" day. Observing the 100th day of the school year was one way that the teachers taught the concept of grouping ones into groups of ten and groups of ten into a group of one hundred. This prepared students for introduction to place value and multiplication in a way that was fun and allowed for physical involvement as well as visual representation of the concepts being taught.

Many speech therapists teach prepositions to students with ASD by having the students get "under" the table, sit "on" the chair, or put the crayon "in" the crayon box. The kinesthetic (motor) involvement of the student in addition to the visual cue and spoken word provides the student with three different sensory avenues in processing a concept, making it more likely to be retained.

When choosing manipulatives, you will want to consider how distracted your student may become when using them. If they are too much fun to play with, they may not be a good choice. You could consider, however, allowing the child to play with them after using them appropriately for instruction.

For children who have difficult with symbol/object correspondence, you can use the actual item so that what is being represented is clear to the child. For example, you might be working on this word problem:

> Jenny had 7 DVDs.
> Then, she gave 1 to her friend.
> How many does she have left?

In this case, it might be helpful to use actual DVDs to represent the number in the math problem. The process of subtraction is represented in a way that is meaningful to the learner.

Mnemonics

A mnemonic is a device or technique, such as a rhyme, acronym, or picture, consciously used as an aid in remembering specific information. For example, you may have learned the mnemonic "Roy G. Biv" to remember the colors in a rainbow (**R**ed, **O**range, **Y**ellow, **G**reen, **B**lue, **I**ndigo, **V**iolet). This is an acronym (you use the first letters of the key words to make a new word or words that will be easier to remember). Likewise, Jed Baker uses mnemonics to teach social skills rules to children with ASD (2003). One example is "using your HEAD during a conversation." The acronym HEAD stands for **H**appy voice, **E**ye contact, **A**lternate, and **D**istance, which are critical aspects of maintaining a social interaction.

Mnemonics can be paired with pictures—for example, a picture of a spring to remember to spring forward (or move the clocks ahead) during the spring and a person falling backward to remember to turn the clocks back in the fall. Pictures can also be linked with word play to help in jogging memory. For example, students may be taught to visualize a "mini soda" to remember the state of Minnesota when studying the United States.

Pictures and Photos

In general, the Internet, for those of you who love to surf, is a rich source of pictures and photos to use in making visual supports. You can search either by topic area, or search for "visual supports" or "visual strategies" as the overall topic area. Use the search engine to search for the topics by typing in the picture you are looking for, plus the word "image." For example, if you are searching for a picture of a dog, you would type "dog images" and hit the return or "go" button.

There are also many clip art software options wherever computer software is sold. You can take your own pictures and make them individualized with your own film or digital camera. In addition, you can buy software "libraries" of images commonly used in making communication boards, picture schedules, etc. One example is the *Picture This* CD-Rom by Silver Lining Media.

Boardmaker™ is a well-known software product designed by the Mayer-Johnson company. According to the manufacturer, it has about 10,000 Picture Communication Symbols© available in 40 languages, so it might be useful when working with a student from a bilingual family. (Picture Communication Symbols are simple line drawings that do not always look exactly like the object they stand for, so the student must be taught their meanings.)

For a good discussion of considerations in choosing pictures appropriate for a given student, we recommend the book *Teaching by Design* by Kim Voss (Woodbine House, 2006).

Picture Exchange Communication System™

The Picture Exchange Communication System™ (PECS) was designed by Andy Bondy and Lori Frost (1994) as an augmentative communication system for students with ASD. PECS, in other words, becomes the student's mode of communication in combination with any other communicative efforts (verbal language, gestures, etc.).

PECS is taught in a specific and systematic format and focuses on the individual with ASD learning to initiate a communication exchange. A child who is using this method learns to gain the attention of the person she is communicating with and then hand him or her a single picture or a series of pictures arranged in a sentence strip. For instance, in the early stages of learning PECS, the child might hand over a picture of a video to indicate that she wants to watch the video, or a picture of a granola bar to indicate she wants a snack. Later, she would learn to put the symbol for "I want" in front of the picture of the granola bar to communicate she wants a snack. This practice mirrors successful verbal communication between two persons.

Students who are already using PECS are well prepared for the use of pictures as a visual support. They are using pictures to communicate, which demonstrates understanding of the pictures themselves. Adults can take advantage of this learned behavior to obtain more independent performance of a variety of skills. For example, a picture of silverware can be placed outside of a kitchen drawer to indicate correct placement of utensils when unloading the dishwasher. A picture of an index finger placed in front of a mouth can indicate that it is time to be quiet. With the addition of the visual cue, the student can learn to be less reliant on an adult to perform some of the activities during the school day or at home.

■ Power Cards™

Power Cards™ were developed by Elisa Gagnon specifically for students with Asperger's syndrome or autism. They were designed in order to take advantage of these students' strong interests as a means of motivating behavior change. For example, if you are working with a student who really enjoys Dungeons and Dragons, you could use characters from the game to model certain social rules such as not interrupting someone in the middle of a conversation. The elf could represent the desired behavior of changing topics with a conversation partner and the dwarf could represent the undesired behavior of sticking to the same topic regardless of the conversation partner's interest.

Typically, Power Cards are small (business card size) and are intended for use by children who read. Cards contain a representative picture and list the steps involved in following the rule being taught. Although Power Cards were intended for older students who are readers, you could adapt the idea by making the cards larger and eliminating the written words as long as the picture clearly represents the concept being taught. According to Elisa Gagnon, Power Cards are not an appropriate option for all people with ASD. They may not be well designed to meet the needs of students who have multiple learning challenges or who are quite unmotivated to engage in the learning environment.

For many students, using a favorite topic provides the motivation to participate in the lesson. Power Cards have been used successfully by both parents and educators. Due to their small size, they can easily be used in a variety of environments and can be carried in a wallet or security card holder, or they can be laminated and placed on a keychain. An example of a Power Card can be seen in Figure 3.18 on page 36.

Sign Language

Sign language has long been used as an augmentative communication system for people with ASD. Hand signals that represent a word or concept are used individually or in combination the same ways we use verbal speech. The purpose of this book is not to teach the reader to use sign language. If you are working with someone who uses signs as her primary means of communication, you are most likely already signing to her as well as responding to her signs.

Sign language can be a discrete way of signaling a certain response to a child in a group situation without disrupting the group or calling attention to the individual. For example, the sign for "quiet" (index and middle finger of both hands crossed in front of the mouth, then moved away) can remind a student to sit quietly during a lesson. If a student has difficulty with receptive language, the use of a sign along with the spoken word can help her to respond more consistently. Please check our reference list at the end of the book for sign language resources.

Social Skills Picture Books

Social Skills Picture Books were first developed by Jed Baker (2002), based on the concept that students with ASD can learn social skills best when a visual model is used. His first book depicts the right and wrong way to do over thirty social skills. Although the book contains pre-established pictures, Dr. Baker strongly recommends that students develop their own books of photos to make the learning experience more meaningful. If you have access to a digital camera, you can easily develop individual stories for the students you are working with.

At the Douglass Developmental Disabilities Center, high school students with Asperger's syndrome are serving as models for a new social skills picture book by Dr. Baker that is geared toward adolescents and adults. The students model both the correct and incorrect way to behave in a social situation, which is augmented by cartoon bubbles that state the accompanying language for each situation.

Social Stories™

Social Stories™ were first developed by Carol Gray, a teacher of students with autism (1991). The goal of a Social Story is to develop in picture/word format, a story about the appropriate use of a target social skill or rule. The story should be written in language geared to the child's abilities. Using pictures in a story format can be useful for students who learn best when information is presented visually. Pictures can be photos, home-made cartoon drawings, etc. Some examples of topics covered by Carol Gray's Social Stories include rules when riding in a vehicle, how to initiate a play interaction, and understanding the concept of emotions.

You can use the Social Stories already written in one of Carol Gray's products or develop one more specific to your child. The stories can be written by an adult with the assistance of a child or by the student alone. Visit Carol Gray's website at www.thegraycenter.org for more information about the use of this visual tool.

Video Modeling

Video modeling involves videotaping one or more people modeling the behavior(s) you want to teach. Video modeling research has demonstrated that some students with autism learn better from a video model than a live model (Charlop-Christy, Le, & Freeman 2000; Haring, Kennedy, Adams, & Pitts-Conway 1987). Research has also demonstrated that the skills learned are maintained over time (Corbett 2003). Once again, this type of technology is readily available to teachers and parents. Digital versions can be stored on CD, allowing for multiple videos to be collected using minimal storage space.

Video modeling can be used to model more complex behavior that cannot be readily depicted in a stationary picture. For example, video modeling can be used to teach: social skills (such as initiating a conversation), performing a critical life skill (such as using an inhaler), and non-interactive skills such as toy use. The options are virtually limitless.

It is helpful for the models to be of the same age as the student who will view the video. If this is not possible, using models who are not the same age (including adults) can be effective. For example, one teacher used a video model to teach preschool students with ASD to clean up after playtime. Even though adults were used as models, the students enjoyed viewing the video, imitated much of the language used in it, and eventually began developing their own verbal responses when performing the actual cleanup activity.

If you know a child who enjoys watching videos and television, this may be a great learning tool.

How Visual Supports Can Help with the Development of Language

A Rutgers University graduate student, working towards certification in special education, described her experience in attempting to teach students with autism the concept of germs in an effort to reduce the spread of illness in her classroom. She was able to teach some of her students to cover their mouths when coughing or sneezing. Regardless of her efforts, there was evidence that the overall concept was still missing as most of the students followed covering their mouths with immediately touching classroom materials and peers, therefore continuing to spread germs.

This teacher had the clever idea of making the vocabulary word germ more concrete by introducing a visual support. She reviewed her previous instructions about the spread of germs and proceeded to sneeze into her hand, which was covered in glitter. She asked the students to think about the glitter as germs, which they cannot ordinarily see, and went on her way throughout the day with her regular instruction. Each student was given glitter to place in their hands when they needed to sneeze or cough and by the end of the day, the students were left with a visual picture of where the germs were in the classroom. They left for the day with the classroom filled with glitter, but with a new understanding of a concept that they could not grasp without the aid of visual supports.

Acquiring language is a much more complex process than one might initially imagine. Language skills are comprised of many different sub-skills, including:

- ***Language comprehension, or the understanding of the spoken word.***
  Many of us refer to this as receptive language. Language comprehension

consists of *semantics*, the understanding of the meaning of a word, and *phonology*, the ability to process word sounds. For example, if you gave a student the instruction to "Sit," he would have to be able to understand what sit means as well as to hear the individual sounds of "s," "i," and "t," so that that word sounded the same each time it was heard.

- *Language expression, the ability to use language to communicate with others.* Although that sounds quite simple, it involves many skills.
  - A learner must have an understanding of *syntax*, which is word order or following grammatical rules. An adult with autism who is employed as a custodian made the following statement: "Ants in the apple. Garbage. Bite it." Only the job coach who accompanied him on that day would be readily able to recognize this as a statement about the day when they found ants feasting on an apple in the garbage.

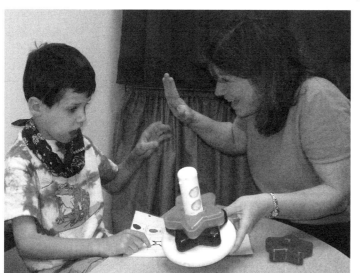

  - It also includes *discourse*, the ability to sequence larger volumes of language such as when relating a past event or giving directions. For example, a child who has difficulties with syntax may be very excited about a family trip to the zoo, but when asked about what he saw or did, he is unable to recount many or all aspects of the event.
  - Expressive language also includes *pragmatics*. Pragmatic language is the understanding of how to use language in a socially appropriate way. It requires an understanding of the give and take of a language interaction as well as sensitivity to the needs of the person you are communicating with. We work with a teenager with Asperger's syndrome who had no reservations about speaking his mind. If he didn't like your hair, he would tell you. If he thought you were overweight, you would hear about it. If he was shopping in the mall and didn't like the looks of the passersby, he would loudly comment, causing bad feelings and potential danger. You can see why pragmatic language is so important, particularly in the community.

Qualitative impairment in communication is part of the diagnostic criteria for autism. It is not an understatement that this area of learning will present significant challenges to our learners. Difficulties in communication skills may often be associated with a wide array of challenging behaviors, such as aggression, self-injury, and tantrums. As a result, it is critical to address this skill area. We have worked with many people with ASD of various ages whose skill development increased exponentially once they were able to effectively make their needs and wants known.

There are many visually based communication systems used to increase and improve language in children with autism. These include PECS, language boards, high tech augmentative communication devices, sign language, and more. It is beyond the scope of this book to describe how to use these individual systems. The strategies described in this book were chosen as a sampling of the supports that could be used. The format can be modified to fit other visually based communication systems.

VISUALIZE THIS: IDEAS, IDEAS, IDEAS

Language Comprehension

Semantics

Children with autism may develop appropriate language, but may have trouble understanding word meanings. Abstract concepts such as idioms can be confusing to them. For example, if a child with autism is told to "stay on your toes," he may take the statement literally rather than understanding it means to stay alert.

Graphic Organizers

As Chapter 2 explains, graphic organizers are useful for students with ASD because they can be used to visually display and organize ideas and concepts. They can be especially helpful in teaching about the meanings of words and expressions.

Figure 3.1 shows how a common phrase can be substituted with different expressions that mean the same thing. In the example shown, the phrase the child un-

Fig. 3.1

derstands (i.e., "what's new?") is located centrally in the organizer and can be highlighted with bold print or color. The branches off this central phrase or idea show how this idea can be represented in several different and perhaps abstract ways.

Another example shows how the concepts "clean" and "dirty" can be visually represented in a graphic organizer. This can be used to show the difference between clean and dirty dishes, clothing, or even a bedroom. Although some students cannot read the words written under the pictures, they can be added or removed depending upon the student's abilities.

Fig. 3.2

Graphic organizers can also be used to help older students grasp abstract concepts such as they might encounter in a social studies class. See, for example, the graphic organizer in Figure 3.3 on the next page, which explains presidential responsibilities.

Thinking Stories

Being able to understand that others may think differently than you is referred to as "Theory of Mind" (Frith, 1989). It is the ability to imagine that other people have thoughts, feelings, or opinions. Many students with autism experience difficulty with this concept that may lead to problems in communicating effectively with others.

Thinking Stories are an advanced form of the Social Story™ (Gray, 1994) described in Chapter 2. They are used to help the individual determine what people are thinking and feeling. They incorporate picture symbols, similar to those used in Comic Strip Conversation (Gray, 1994). The symbols illustrate phrases, behaviors, or social misunderstandings. The example in Figure 3.4 on the next page uses a Thinking Story which highlights the unfamiliar phrase and then provides several potential explanations about what the speaker might be trying to communicate.

Fig. 3.3

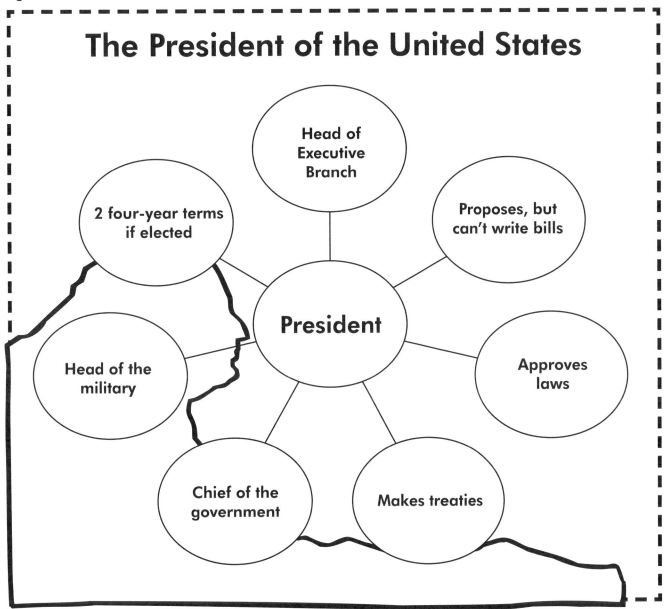

Fig. 3.4

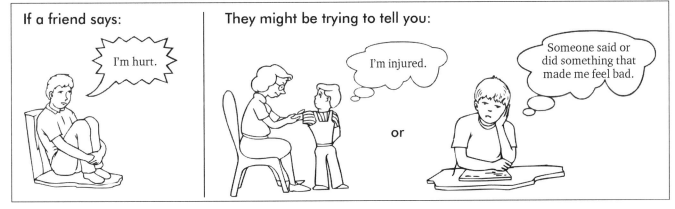

Some children need concrete examples to support their parent's request to follow hygiene routines such as to shower and use deodorant daily. When given a visual support that illustrates rules with sound, sensible explanations to support these requests, some children may follow rules with less resistance. Likewise, Thinking Stories can be used to explain common requests such as "pick up your dirty clothes." Some children may find it easier to comply with demands if they are given justification for the request. (See Figures 3.5 and 3.6 below.)

Fig. 3.5

When mom says:

Do your laundry.

She asks me to do this job because:

The laundry hamper is full.

The bedroom smells bad.

There are no clean clothes.

Fig. 3.6

Mom  says:

"Do your laundry."

She asks me to do this job because:

The laundry hamper is full.

The bedroom smells bad.

There are no clean clothes.

Sign Language

Some people with ASD have difficulty understanding verbal language. They may experience challenges in responding to, and comprehending verbal directions. As Chapter 2 discusses, using sign language along with verbal language can provide the learner with a cue that may improve language acquisition.

Sign language can provide visual cues to supplement auditory stimuli (verbal direction). There are several ways to use sign language to help augment a student's understanding of the spoken word.

Simultaneous Communication. Parents, teachers, and friends can help learners focus on the key phrases spoken by pairing sign language with spoken words (simultaneous communication). As a speaker gives the direction "sit down," he or she should simultaneously use the sign for "sit." All verbal directions should be paired with the coordinating sign. This strategy can also be used to teach the names of different objects in the environment.

Emphasizing Prepositions. Prepositions can be confusing to students with autism. Provide the sign language cue to highlight the preposition when giving directions. For example, if the direction is "Put the book under the desk," the teacher should sign only the word "under." Pairing the sign with the preposition adds a visual cue to make this skill easier to learn.

Using Signs with Other Visual Supports. When teaching a new sign, a chart or poster with a photograph of the object or action, plus a picture of someone modeling the sign may help the child make the connection between the word or object and the manual sign. If you are teaching a student a verb (for example, brush hair), the poster can have photographs of the object, someone demonstrating the action, and another picture of the person modeling the sign.

Provide visual supports for the student as well as for everyone else who interacts with him. Make posters for the home and the classroom showing commonly used signs with a corresponding picture. This will make it easier for everyone to remember to use total communication (speaking as you sign), as well as to model the accurate use of sign language. A small photo album can be filled with signs and given to the child to use as a reference guide. See Figures 3.7a-b on the next page.

▇ Phonology

If the student has trouble producing words, it may be due to difficulties remembering how the mouth should be shaped or formed in order to produce specific sounds. For some students, it can be helpful to use a mirror so the child can see himself and the teacher modeling the correct movement. Although the teacher can model the sound and the proper movements, this cue is temporary and cannot be referred to again. The visual supports discussed below are permanent and available to the student at all times.

Flashcards or Charts

Use flashcards or charts that provide a visual representation of what position the mouth and lips must be in to make different sounds. These flashcards can be purchased or you can make your own with the help of a speech therapist. On each

Fig. 3.7a   **Fig. 3.7b**

Brush

Brush hair

card have a photograph of the mouth making the sound, a picture of an object, and the letters that correspond with the sound. A card representing "lollipop" would have the letter "L" with a picture of a lollipop and a photograph of a mouth making the "L" sound. See Figure 3.8 below.

Sometimes, children with ASD can formulate the proper oral motor movements in isolation but have difficulty when putting all the sounds together to form

Fig. 3.8

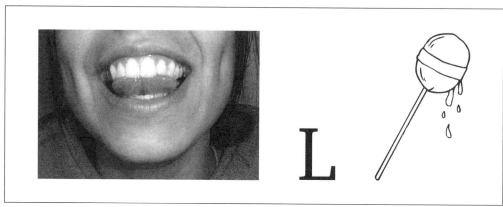

a word. In this case single flashcards for each component sound in a specific word can be paired together to show the formation of the word. In the example shown in Figures 3.9a-c, the word bath is broken down into the three phonetic sounds that make up the word. The child can see how each letter sound is formed. If the child consistently leaves the last sound off words, provide him with small cue cards. The word can be written on the card with the last sound highlighted. For simple flashcards you can glue prints of photos to index cards and/or you can print out digital photos on regular paper or photo paper and glue to a stiffer backing or laminate.

Fig. 3.9a

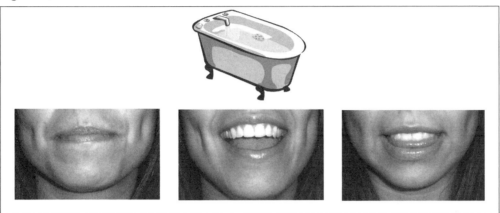

Fig. 3.9b

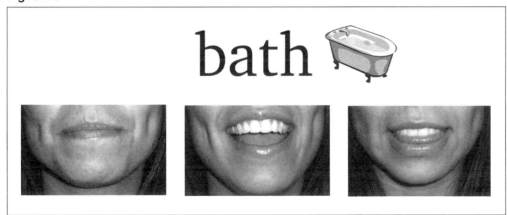

Fig. 3.9c

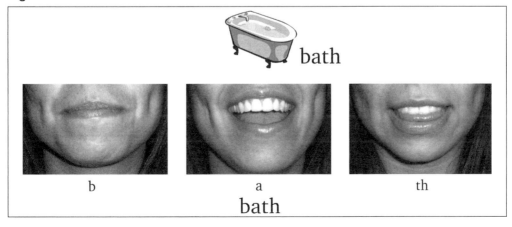

■ Language Expression

Syntax

Although most listeners will understand the request "Chicken, more, I want," the grammatical arrangement of these words is incorrect. To communicate effectively with others, it is important to consistently use proper syntax. Use the following suggestions to teach students with ASD about word order.

Syntax Flip Books

You can create a flip book that requires no reading ability. It uses line drawings representing different parts of a sentence (subjects, verbs, objects, and prepositional phrases). The pictures are assembled in a bound book (or loose leaf binder) that enables each sentence element to be flipped independently of one another. This feature enables the user to create a variety of combinations as well as control the complexity of each sentence. It also can address plural nouns, possessives, pronouns, and past and present tenses. See Figures 3.10 – 3.12 for an example of a subject, verb, object sentence structure. The parent or teacher can adapt the complexity of syntax used by flipping a blank card over part of the complete sentence.

Fig. 3.10

Colored Block or Dot Cues

Figure 3.13 (color insert) shows how a teacher can place an additional cue of a colored block to highlight the different elements of the sentence when teaching the parts of

Fig. 3.11

Fig. 3.12

speech. (Orange blocks represent the subject; purple the verb; yellow the object; and green, prepositional phrases.) In the beginning stages of sentence development, the student can take the blocks and place them on the individual pictures

Over time, the teacher can gradually fade the student's reliance on the blocks by printing the subject in orange, the verb in purple, and the object in yellow (Figure 3.14, color insert). The font size should be slowly decreased as the student becomes more proficient at proper sentence structure. Then the colored words can be changed one by one to black (the color of most printed material).

Caterpillar Organizers

This suggestion to improve syntax may appeal to younger children who know how to read. This variation of a graphic organizer uses a caterpillar with different body segments; each segment represents a part of a sentence (subject, verb, object). The caterpillar can be as short as two sections or even longer depending upon the complexity of the sentence structure. Color each segment to correlate to the corresponding sentence element. The colors used for each part of speech can be selected by the parent or teacher, but should stay consistent throughout instruction.

An entire class can create these sentence caterpillars, then cut them apart and use them interchangeably to create new sentences. Keep in mind that although the sentence order may be correct, nonsense sentences may be created. See Figure 3.15 in the color insert for an example.

Written Sentence Strips

In order to build independence in using full sentences, you can create sentence strips.

Type or handwrite the sentence on an index card or piece of paper. Then cut out each word and glue a piece of Velcro to the back. Cut out a long strip of paper that is slightly wider than your word cards and long enough for you to place all your word cards on it in sentence order. Glue the other side of the Velcro to this strip. Begin by placing the words in the correct order on the strip. Later, remove words systematically from the strip and see if the child can fill in the blanks. Gradually remove more words until no words are present on the strip. Each time you remove an additional word, make sure the child can still say the complete sentence (or can put the words back on the sentence strip in the right order). Eventually, remove the blank strip as well. This strategy helps a child to develop a visual pattern of the words used in correct syntactical format.

Discourse

Many students with autism are unable to maintain conversations. They can answer simple questions, but do not know how to sustain a conversation. They find it difficult to communicate beyond the level of simple phrases.

Graphic Organizers

Graphic organizers can help people with ASD organize their thoughts so they can actively participate in conversations and build upon existing skills. For example, the person can create a new graphic organizer before placing a phone call to a friend or relative. He can fill in the branches of the organizer prior to the conversation so he can individualize the organizer depending on the listener. For recurring events such as calling the pizzeria to order a meal, the graphic organizer can be filled in with information the speaker will always need to provide (e.g., give your name/phone number/what you are ordering).

If a student will be talking to someone about a trip or perhaps giving a presentation for a school project, a graphic organizer can help him capture all of his ideas in a systematic fashion. See Figure 3.16 for an example of a telephone conversation with a new friend.

Fig. 3.16

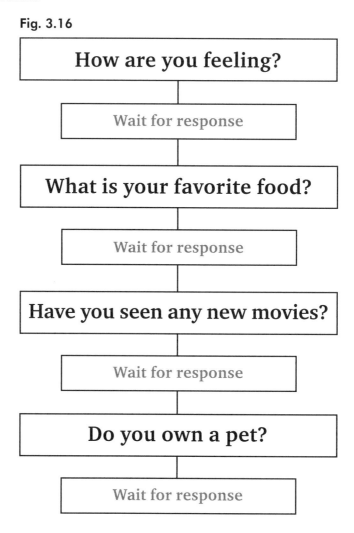

Picture Cues

Have you ever asked a student with autism to tell you what he did at school? Did he struggle with an answer? It is not unusual for children and adults with autism to have trouble recalling past events. They may be motivated to discuss the events of the day but can only remember a small part, or sometimes are unable to produce any answer.

You can help the student recall events needed to carry on a conversation by providing him with a photo album or a wallet with pictures of the event. Take photographs of him doing the activity. A digital camera will come in handy here to reduce the delay in the creation of the book and actual event. The student should be an active participant in the creation of the book. Once you have taken the photographs, place them in a small album or wallet or on a simple metal ring. Postcards purchased while on vacation can also be used.

Short written descriptions can accompany the photographs. Individualize the wording depending upon the person's reading ability. You can write full sentences for a child who is a good reader, or short, simple phrases that will help him get the conversation started. (See Figure 3.17.) For students who have no reading ability, the picture alone will be the cue for different topics to talk about. Some students may need to rely on the written word to maintain a conversation. Think of professionals who use Power Point or similar visual displays to give presentations. Some people rely fully on those tools, while others use them merely as a guide.

Fig. 3.17

I went to the San Diego Zoo with my mom and dad.

The panda bear was black and white. He ate bamboo.

I saw an orangutan. It was big and had orange hair.

Pragmatics

It is important for all children and adults with autism to understand and use language appropriately in social contexts. Some people may forget how to initiate and sustain conversations. Others require clarification about social events they may encounter or conversations that they had and did not fully understand. The following suggestions may help students who have difficulty in this area.

Power Cards™

Power Cards™, developed by Elisa Gagnon (2001), use special interests to motivate students with autism. Power Cards are most often used with students who can read, but parents and teachers can adapt them for use with nonreaders, as long as the pictures used clearly represent the concept you are teaching. Power Cards can help an individual increase appropriate conversational topics. In addition, Power Cards can help children understand language related to abstract concepts.

Power Cards can be made in a smaller, business-card size for a child to keep in his pocket or carry in a wallet, or they can be attached to a desk. Adding a photograph or drawing to the card will make it more attractive to the student. The example shown in Figure 3.18 is designed to help the student remember how to initiate and maintain a conversation. Refer to Chapter 2 for more information on using Power Cards.

Fig. 3.18

Astro Man likes to talk with different people. He has to keep the conversation interesting and remember not to focus only on his interests. Sometimes he gets nervous, so he follows these tips to get started.

1. Start the conversation by saying "Hello."
2. Then ask, "Would you like to talk?"
3. There are a lot of different topics I can talk about, but pick just one.
4. Some good topics are:
   - What did you do last night?
   - Do you have any plans for the weekend?
   - What kind of music do you like?
   - Do you have any pets?
   - What is you favorite food?

If the person I am talking to says they have to go, I should say, "Thanks for talking to me" and then let them leave.

Video Modeling

Video modeling can be used to teach students how to engage appropriately in conversations in almost any social context. New videos can be created based upon the individual needs of the student. Video models are appropriate for all learners regardless of their age or their reading ability. The videos are usually very short in length and clearly demonstrate the desired behavior. For example, if you wanted to help a child maintain appropriate conversation while at a party, you would role play with several other people some conversations that might occur in a party situation. The "actors" in the video would be as close in age to the child as possible and would engage in sample conversations. See Chapter 2 for more information about this technique.

Social Stories™

Social Stories™ (Gray, 1994) are simple short stories focusing on social situations that may be difficult for the person with ASD to understand. For example, stories might be written to help someone understand how to make appropriate conversation in the classroom, at a party, or even while attending a funeral. Social Stories can help students understand that conversation topics change depending upon the situation. The stories, which are authored by parents and teachers, should be written in language that the learner comprehends.

Social Stories should be read by the student and reviewed with a parent or teacher often to reinforce the skill area being developed. For students who cannot read, the parent or teacher can read the story aloud and review the concept with the student. Many students benefit from the addition of photographs or drawings in the story.

Comic Strip Conversations™

Comic Strip Conversations™ (Gray, 1994) turn abstract conversations into concrete visual representation. They can be used to help a child with ASD understand social situations, solve problems, or clarify conversations that occur in the past, present, or future.

Comic Strip Conversations use basic symbols that represent different components of conversation (talk, listen, thoughts, loud and quiet). New symbols can be created for individual students. Colors are also incorporated into the comic strip conversation to indicate the intended emotion of the speaker. The words are colored depending upon their content. For example, facts are in black, and angry statements are in red. In the example in Figure 3.19 (color insert), words that are spoken aloud are indicated with a different kind of thought balloon than thoughts that are not spoken.

Although there are some similarities between Comic Strip Conversations and Social Stories, the main purpose of Comic Strip Conversations is to show the actual conversation between two or more characters and offer some insight into what the characters may be thinking. A Social Story may contain script, but also contains an explanation of the expectations for a particular social situation.

Fig.9.11

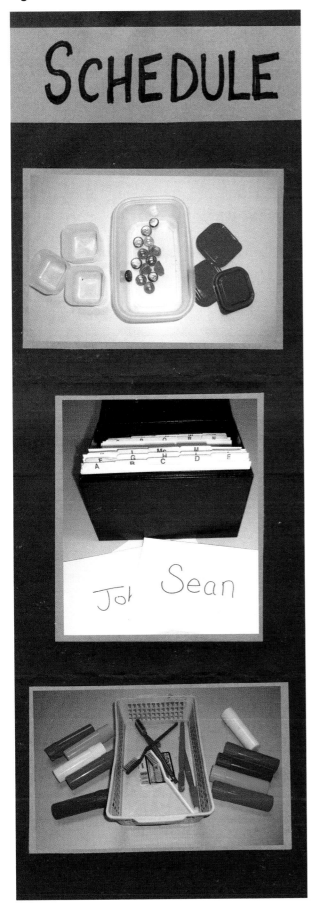

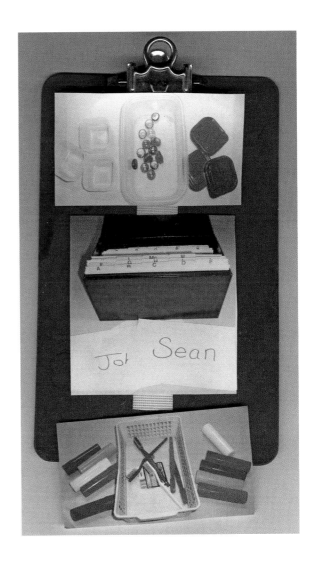

Fig.9.4

Fig.9.7

$6 \times 4 =$ $6 \times 4 =$ $6 \times 4 =$

$8 + 7 =$ $8 + 7 =$ $8 + 7 =$

$15 - 6 =$ $15 - 6 =$ $15 - 6 =$

Mrs. Lindley

ART
Room 121

4

Using Visual Supports to Increase Memory
The Who, What, Where, Why, and How

Jason, a ten-year-old with autism, could tell time using a digital clock, but was having a great deal of difficulty learning to read an analog clock commercially designed for instruction. Jason's mother, home programmer, and school staff had tried using a verbal prompt (e.g., "four th____" to prompt the response four thirty), but were unable to fade it effectively. They thought about using a visual prompt (the digital time written on a cue card), but were unsure about how to fade out the prompt.

We decided that Jason would need to first associate the digital time (something he already knew) with the analog time (something he had to learn). Jason had a tendency to become frustrated by new tasks in general and we thought that this would help to lessen the frustration. After he was able to make the association between the digital and analog time (using a flashcard at the base of the analog clock), we began to fade the stimulus prompt by placing a sheet of wax paper over the flashcard. We systematically placed additional pieces of wax paper over the visual cue until the time was unreadable. Eventually, we were able to get rid of the flashcard all together.

Jason is now so comfortable with his ability to read time (both analog and digital) that he can spontaneously read the time on the clock in any room and associate that with transitions to new tasks. Jason is truly an example of "Where there is a will, there is a way."

This is a chapter that we can all relate to. We all use some type of visual cues to help us remember who a person is (a name plate or name badge); what we need to purchase (a shopping list); when we need to do something (a calendar); where we need to go (a map); why we need to do or not do something (a picture of the lungs of a smoker); and how to do something (perhaps those annoying installation instructions that come with a new printer cartridge). So, it should not be surprising that students with autism also require visual supports to help them successfully get through the day.

Memory is actually much more complex than one might think. According to David Sousa (2001), in order to get information into long-term memory (for the information that needs to be retained), it has to go through several steps:

- First, information must pass through your **sensory register,** your neurological filter indicating what is important/not important to attend to. This is an area that people with autism may have difficulty with. Perhaps you have tried to teach a skill to a child with autism who was attending to the candy wrapper being opened in the other room or the reflection of light coming from the television, window, or microwave. Her sensory register was not blocking out the stimuli irrelevant to learning the skill and, as a result, she was not able to process the information into memory. Think about a coffee filter with a hole in it. What we want to see is the brewed coffee, but instead we get coffee grinds as well. Once you take that first mouthful, you discard the cup of coffee (including the grinds) and so that pot of coffee becomes unusable.

- Next, information that does pass successfully through the sensory register moves into **working memory.** This is the point when your brain determines whether the information is useful. If the information is determined not to be useful, it is not processed further. Students with autism who do not understand why they need to learn a particular skill will have difficulty in this part of the memory process. Information must make sense and have meaning to the learner. This is why it is important to teach skills that have functional relevance to the student.

- After successfully making it through the working memory, information moves to **short-term memory.** This involves remembering facts that are important now, but not necessarily later. To remember a phone number that will be needed now, but not later, would not require storing it in long-term memory. Often, the person who is teaching the student with ASD has to help her decide whether the information will be necessary at a later time. If so, the teacher will have to make sure the student practices the information in order for it to be processed into long-term memory.

- **Long-term memory** involves remembering information that is important both now and later. Skills taught at home or in an educational setting as part of the instructional plan fall into this category. One thing we know about children with ASD is that they might lose skills that are not practiced. For many students with autism, this indicates the need for extended school year programming. Think about the things that we still remember from our educational experience, such as our number facts, long and sort vowel sounds, object labels. How are we still able to remember these things today? It is most likely because we practiced these skills over and over and over again. For students with autism who are being taught skills that are critical to future functioning, repetition and practice becomes even more critical.

■ Lastly, information must be **organized in the brain** so that it can be readily accessed at a later date. Think about memory as a filing cabinet that is organized with file folders that are further organized into hanging files. If you have ever used such a filing system, you can probably remember times when you were frustrated because you could not find the file you needed. This has much to do with how carefully you filed the information in the first place. Sometimes students with autism may have stored information into long-term memory, but are not able to locate it or to locate it efficiently when it is needed.

This chapter will provide information that can help children and adults with ASD remember:
  ■ Who (using name badges, name tents, name plaques, and signs);
  ■ What (using color coding, confronting oneself with the stimuli, "To Do" or job chore lists, shopping lists, fact tables, Post-It notes, concept maps and graphic organizers, homework folders, and memory plans);
  ■ Where (using cues for the correct orientation of clothing during dressing, cues to identify a locker/cubby/materials, labels to indicate where personal items are stored, and seating charts);
  ■ Why (using pictures for concept development, social stories or visual cards, concept maps and graphic organizers); and
  ■ How (using written or picture instructions/diagrams, a checklist or picture sequence to perform a complex skill, and scratch paper)

Note: The concept of "when" is addressed in Chapter 5.

VISUALIZE THIS: IDEAS, IDEAS, IDEAS

■ Who????

There are several visual strategies to use if a student with ASD is having difficulty remembering names. Some basic solutions include having the people in the learner's environment wear nametags or posting their names on the doors of their office in the school. In addition to posting names, it may be helpful to give as many pieces of information about that person as would help to identify "who" they are and what they do at the school. For example, it may be helpful to attach a small photograph of the individual. Some children may be able to recognize the school nurse, but not know his/her name.

Fig. 4.1

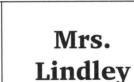

Name Tent

Name tents are helpful tools in a classroom where the child has to remember the names of several peers. Take a piece of heavy construction paper and fold it in half lengthwise. Using crayons or markers, have each student write his or her name on one side. Display the name tents on the corner of the student's desk. If the student cannot read, photo cards can be substituted (see below).

Photo Cards

Some middle or high school students may have more than one teacher. It may be challenging to remember the names of these teachers and what subject they teach. Photo cards—small cards that can be placed on the inside of a notebook or in a wallet—can be used as a quick reference to remember names.

To make photo cards, obtain a small photograph of each teacher. Glue the photograph on a piece of heavy paper (about the size of a business card). Then write the teacher's name, the subject he or she teaches, and the class number on the card. Laminate the cards for durability. (See Figure 4.1.)

Graphic Organizers

When a child is learning to read books and has difficulty remembering the characters, a separate graphic organizer can be used to help. The illustration in Figure 4.2 is an example of a graphic organizer developed for *The Adventures of Amelia Bedelia.*

If the book contains pictures, as in those read by younger readers, the pictures of the characters can be used in place of, or in addition to, the text in the graphic organizer.

Fig. 4.2

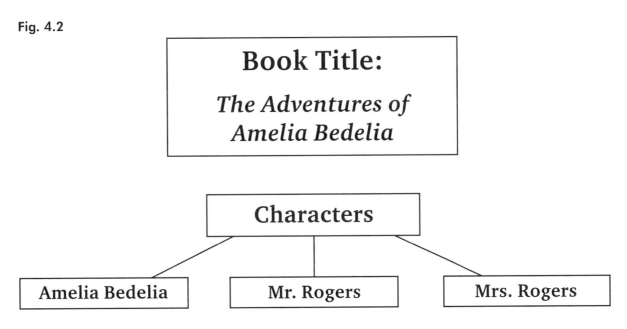

What???

There are two general situations in which students with ASD can benefit from visual strategies to help with remembering "what" information. First, like everyone else, they may have difficulty remembering WHAT they need to do. Our days are filled with many distractions making it challenging to remember what we are supposed to accomplish. Students with autism may face these same obstacles when trying to remember their homework assignments, chores, or which setting to use on a dishwasher.

Second, they may have trouble remembering factual information (WHAT is 7 x 8? WHAT is a mammal?). It is beyond the scope of this book to provide in-depth information about teaching academic content to students with autism, but a few general strategies for visual support are listed below and additional strategies helpful for supporting academic learning are in Chapter 5.

Life Skills Examples

Manila or Pocket Folders

Use a manila folder or a pocket folder to help students remember homework assignments. This strategy works well when the student is given worksheets for homework. On the left side of the folder, place a chart with two columns. In the first column, the student, teacher, or parent can write the assignment. It is helpful to number each assignment and then write the number on the corresponding worksheet. The second column of the chart will be used to indicate when the assignment is completed. The student or parent can place a sticker, smiley face, or check mark in the box when work is finished. Clip the corresponding worksheets to the right side of the folder. (See Figure 4.3.)

Fig. 4.3

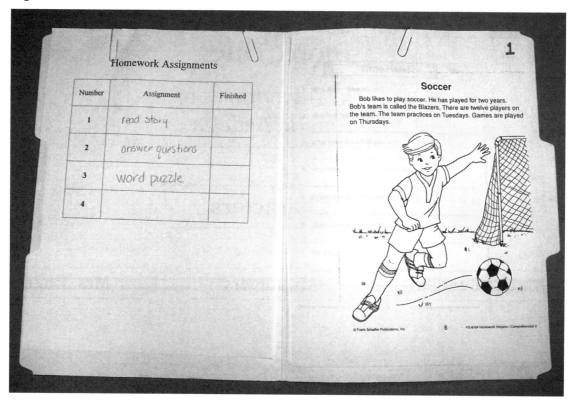

Another way to organize homework is to color code pocket folders by subject (red for Math, blue for English, green for Science). Color coordinate the textbooks and all other materials needed for each subject with colored stickers. This will help the student become more efficient in finding the necessary books to complete class and homework assignments.

Assignment Books

Use a homework assignment book in conjunction with the homework folder. As the student writes down each assignment in her book, she should place a colored sticker that coordinates with the subject (red for Math, blue for English, green for Science) next to her description of the assignment. At a glance, she will be able to determine which books and folders must be taken home to complete her assignments. The particular type of assignment book selected will vary depending on the student's level. It may be best to begin with a daily assignment book. Some individuals will need ongoing instruction on how to use the book; however, for others it is merely a time management tool.

Lists

Having trouble remembering what to pick up at the grocery store is a common problem. The simplest solution is a grocery list. If the individual with ASD cannot write, use picture cards to serve as the grocery list. Take photographs of items she may need to purchase at the grocery store, glue them onto index cards, and then cover them with clear contact paper or laminate to make them more durable. She can carry the photo-shopping list to the grocery store in a small index card box or case. After she has retrieved each item, she can return the corresponding card to the box. See Figures 4.4 to 4.6 for examples.

For nonreaders:

Fig. 4.4

For beginning readers:

Fig. 4.5

crackers

cookies

macaroni

For children who can read and select their own item, depending upon size, brand, flavor, etc.:

Fig. 4.6

CHICKEN

EGGS

SODA

POTATOES

"To-Do" lists come in handy in everyone's life. We make lists to remind ourselves about what we need to do, what we need to buy, and what we need to make. Children or adults with autism may also have difficulty remembering a long list of jobs that need to be completed. Many individuals with ASD benefit from clear, organized lists of activities. The lists can be written and/or be paired with photographs. (See Figures 5.6 and 5.7 for examples.) They may also benefit from learning to use formal activity schedules, as described in Chapter 2.

Color Coding

Colored arrows or dots can be used to indicate appropriate settings for household appliances such as the washer and dryer. The user can learn to match up the colored arrows or dots using the dial and will always have the correct setting for doing her laundry. (See Figure 4.7.)

The correct temperature (cold or hot water) for the type of clothing can also be color-coded. See Figure 4.8 in the color insert for an example for a nonreader and Figure 4.9 in the color insert for an example for a reader.

Does your son or daughter dress himself or herself independently, but use poor judgment when trying to match clothing? A color-coding system may be your solution. You use the colored dots to indicate which items match. For example, a red shirt may match a pair of jeans or a pair of black pants. A red dot placed in an unobtrusive place on the shirt and also on the pants it matches can help the child remember what matches with what.

Fig. 4.7

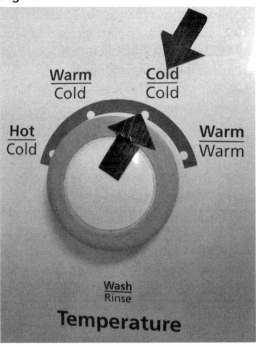

Colored dots may be placed on tags, or, if the child does not like tags in her clothing, you can also use permanent marker or any other means of color-coding (such as colored embroidery thread). Then all the child has to do is match color codes for pants and shirts. Items like blue jeans, which can be worn with virtually any color top, can be multiply color-coded. This strategy can enable students with ASD to achieve true independence without having to memorize all of the rules for coordinating clothing.

Post-It Notes™

After being given verbal directions, some students may need an additional cue. Using Post-It Notes™ to write reminders such as "feed the dog," "go to the store," or "call mom" helps them remember what needs to be completed. The student can carry the notes to school and write reminders about homework assignments that can be placed on the outside of her textbooks.

Objects As Memory Joggers

Some students may forget items they need for school. It may help to confront them with the stimuli. For example, place the items a child needs to remember, such as the mail, gym shoes, or her book bag, near the door. The objects may prompt her to perform the desired response (going to the Post Office, going to the gym, or being prepared for school).

Academic Examples

Number Facts Grid

"Children with severe memory deficits may understand the underlying number system but may be unable to recall number facts quickly" (Lerner, 2003). Number facts grids can make completion of math computations (addition, subtraction, multiplication, and division) more efficient for students with autism. Grids can be attached to the inside of a student's notebook. Good visual learners can often eventually store the grid to memory (like a picture in your head) for future use. See Figure 4.10 for an example of a multiplication grid.

Note: Many more visual supports for math skills are included in the next chapter on Temporal Sequential skills.

Fig. 4.10

X	1	2	3	4	5	6
1	1	2	3	4	5	6
2	2	4	6	8	10	12
3	3	6	9	12	15	18
4	4	8	12	16	20	24
5	5	10	15	20	25	30
6	6	12	16	24	30	36

Number Dots

If a child can already identify written numbers by name, number dots can help her learn how much a numeral stands for. Counting four dots on the number four, for instance, can help her internalize the meaning of four. (See Figure 4.11.) If your child or student does well with number dots, she may benefit from TouchMath—a commercially available, complete method for teaching counting, operations, and money identification using dots. See www.touchmath.com.

Fig. 4.11

Drawings

Homemade drawings, sketches, and cartoons can be used to help students remember various types of academic information. For instance, you can make cartoons to help students remember historical events or science concepts such as the laws of motion.

Drawings can also be used to help children learn how to spell individual words. For example, to teach a child to read the word "car," a picture of a car can be gradually shaped into the letters c a r (see Figure 4.12).

Fig. 4.12

Adapted from: Cooper, Heron, & Heward, 1987

Graphic Organizers

The Venn diagram (a form of graphic organizer) is made up of two or more overlapping circles. As you may recall, the areas where the circles overlap are used to indicate similarities between the people, places, or things being compared.

Venn diagrams can be used in any subject to help a student compare and contrast characteristics. They can be used in Reading or Language Arts to compare characters (their attributes, motivations, etc.); in Social Studies, to compare countries, cultures, traditions, geographical features, etc.; in math to compare attributes of shapes; in Science, to compare differences and similarities in the planets, rocks vs. minerals, plants vs. animals, etc. (See Figure 4.13.)

For nonreaders or students who enjoy using manipulatives, you can make Venn diagrams out of yarn or string circles and then have the student place objects or pictures in the circles to indicate similarities and differences. For example, if you are teaching which animals eat meat, which eat plants, and which eat both (or the words "carnivore," "vegetarian," and omnivore") you can make overlapping string circles for vegetarians and carnivores, and have the student put animal figures or pictures in the correct circles.

Fig. 4.13

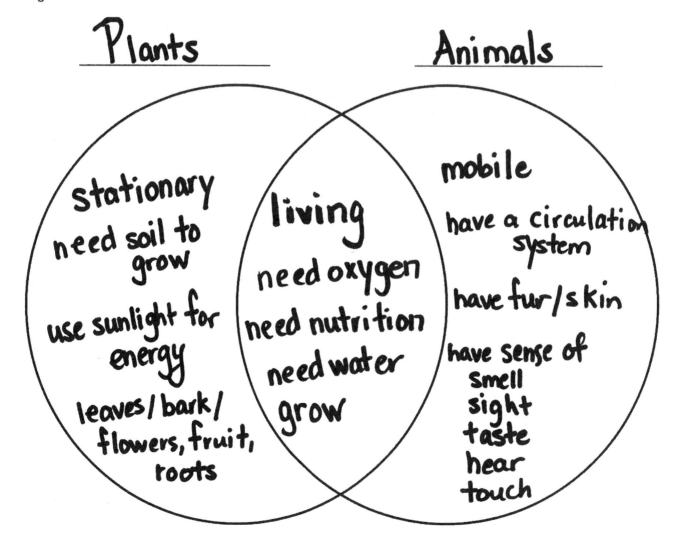

Refer back to Chapter 2 for some basic information on other types of graphic organizers. Some tips for using graphic organizers with students on the autism spectrum include:

- Make sure there is enough room to write.
- Create the organizer on lined paper if the student needs help with spacing her writing.
- Color code graphic organizers to aid in memory. Create a new shape for the organizer that might be more interesting for student.
- Determine how much information you want to include (all or part of the necessary information) before you decide how many balloons, etc. to make for the student to fill in.

Visual Supports for Writing

There are various types of visual supports to help students remember WHAT they need to write. For example, there are structures that can help students remember that when they write a paragraph, they need a topic sentence, two or three supporting details, and then a concluding sentence. For example, many elementary school teachers use the "hamburger" model to help students remember how to write a five-sentence paragraph. They draw or print out a large picture of a cheeseburger with space for sentences to be written in on the drawing: the topic sentence goes in the top bun, supporting details go on the lettuce, cheese, and meat, and the concluding sentence goes on the bottom bun.

A written checklist is another visual support to help students check their own work to make sure they're not leaving something important out or that they proof their work. For example, a proofing checklist might include these questions:

1. Do all my sentences begin with a capital letter?
2. Do all my sentences end with a period or question mark?
3. Did I indent the beginning of my paragraph?

Flashcards

Flashcards can be used to help students memorize academic material. You can use color coding to help categorize information, or add photos, drawings, or icons to the flashcards as memory joggers. For example, when teaching biology, you can color code the organs of the circulatory system red, the skeletal system blue, and digestive system green. Or when teaching which people are in the executive, legislative, and judicial branches of the U.S. government, you can use a different color for each branch. When using flashcards, it is best to work on memorizing smaller chunks of information at a time (e.g., circulatory system, then digestive system, etc.).

▦ Where?????

All of us, with and without ASD, need to know where our belongings go, as well as how to make our way through our environment. Many of the same strategies that help the rest of us know where to put our things can be adapted to help students with autism spectrum disorders.

Fig. 4.14

Seating Charts

Seating charts can help the student visualize her place in the classroom. The seating chart can have written names or photographs of each student in the class. Stickers, nametags, and colored labels placed on the desks can provide another visual cue to help the student find her seat. (See Figures 4.14, 4.15, and 4.16 for examples for nonreaders, beginning readers, and readers, respectively.)

Stickers and Labels

Some students may have difficulty remembering which locker or cubby is theirs. When faced with a large number of lockers, it becomes challenging to tell them apart ("Is mine the fourth from the end or is it number four?") Placing a sticker or label on a locker can be helpful. Try to find something the child is interested in (sports teams, cartoons, or cars) and which stands out from the typical stickers. Purchase several stickers (the same style) and place them on the locker, on the student's backpack, and inside her notebook. The stickers on the backpack and notebook will serve as additional reminders and eliminate the need to remember which sticker is hers!

Some children and adults with ASD may not remember where personal items or work materials belong. Suppose a child is emptying a dishwasher and is expected to put all of the items away. If she cannot remember where the pots or dishes belong, this task may be particularly problematic. One solution is to place labels on cabinets, dressers, or storage areas. A photograph of the actual items that are inside the

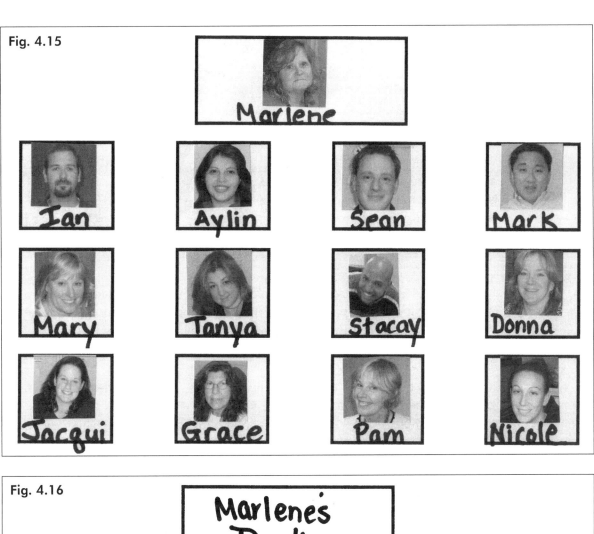

Fig. 4.15

Marlene

Ian   Aylin   Sean   Mark

Mary   Tanya   Stacay   Donna

Jacqui   Grace   Pam   Nicole

Fig. 4.16

Marlene's
Desk

Ian	Aylin	Sean	Mark
Mary	Tanya	Stacay	Donna
Jacqui	Grace	Pam	Nicole

cabinet can be placed on the outer door or drawer (see Figure 4.17). This helps the individual locate items needed and also makes putting items away easier.

Fig. 4.17

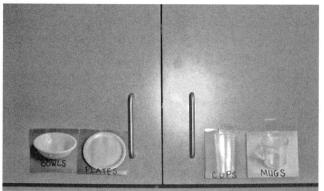

Bins and Baskets

Some people with ASD cannot remember which coat or hat is theirs. Remembering which work materials belongs to them may also prove to be challenging. At home or in the classroom, individual bins or baskets can be used to keep personal belongings organized. Assign each student or family member a different basket or storage bin. Place the person's name, photograph, or other individualized symbol (color coding may be helpful here) on the basket for easy identification. Now, remembering which shoes and mittens are yours on a busy morning will be simple!

Placement Graphics

Drawings, diagrams, and tracings can be used to help students with autism remember where something goes.

For example, place a small graphic of a bare foot inside the shoe to cue the child as to which foot to place in which shoe. The letters "L" and "R" could also be added to give the child additional information, if needed. (See Figure 4.18.)

As an alternative, you could place colored dots or stickers on the inner edge of the insole inside of both shoes. When the shoes are lined up correctly, the dots nearly touch; when they line up incorrectly, the dots are farther apart.

Other ways to use drawings to help the person remember where to put something include table setting, sorting silverware, and organizing work tools. For example, if someone is learning to set the table, you can draw outlines of the knife, fork, and spoon on placemats to show her where to put them.

Fig. 4.18

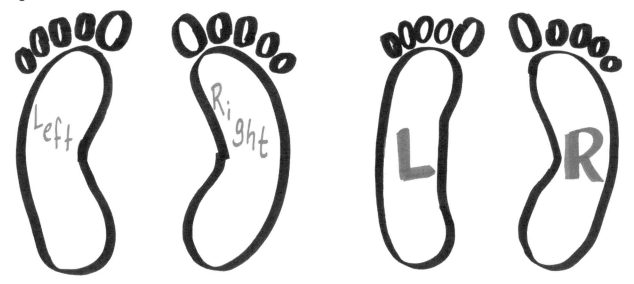

Color Coding

Colors may be used in a variety of ways to cue direction or position. For example, a green dot on the left side of a piece of paper can help a child remember that she should begin writing on that side, and a red dot on the right side can help her remember to stop there.

More sophisticated color coding can help students remember the correct finger positioning that is critical for good keyboarding skills. When learning to type, knowing *where* to place your fingers may be a challenge with so many other distractions on the keyboard. Use color coding to draw attention to where fingers need to be placed on the keyboard for correct typing. Color code the keyboard and create matching cotton gloves with colored fingertips to coordinate with the keys. For example, all the letters that are typed with the left index finger are blue. See Figures 4.19 and 4.20 in the color insert for pictures of the color-coded keyboard and the matching gloves.

■ Why?????

Some children and adults with ASD require explanations for various situations they encounter before they will do as asked. They want to know "why" they need to shower or "why" it is important to do homework. The visual strategies below will be useful to the students who need to know, but who may forget why they have to do certain tasks or behave in certain ways.

Power Cards™

As explained in Chapter 2, Power Cards use a learner's personal interests as a way to capture her attention and build upon skills. The example shown in Figure 4.21 begins with a written scenario that describes the problem. The special interest person ("hero") is used to provide the solution to the problem. The solution can be placed on a small index card or business card that the student carries with her. She can refer back to the card to help remember why it is important to look at someone when speaking. More detailed information on how to use Power Cards can be found in the book *Power Cards* by Elisa Gagnon.

Fig. 4.21

Kelly Clarkson likes to meet her fans. When she gives a concert, she often has an opportunity to meet many of her fans backstage after the show. When Kelly meets someone new, she walks up to them, shakes their hand, and says "hello." Kelly always looks at her fan's eyes so they know she is talking to them.

When you are talking to someone, Kelly wants you to remember why it is important to look at them.

1. You get their attention and keep it.
2. They know you are interested in them.
3. It shows respect.
4. They know you are talking to them.

Fig. 4.22

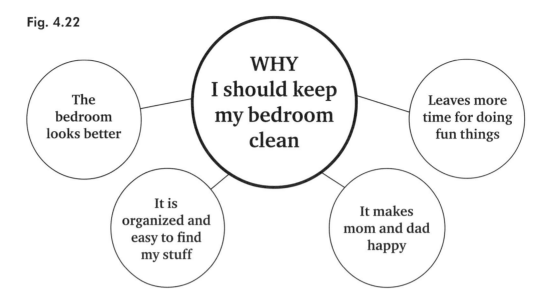

Graphic Organizer

Graphic organizers can be used to remind both readers and nonreaders of reasons they need to do something. For example, the graphic organizer in Figure 4.22 provides a reminder as to why it is important to keep your bedroom clean. It places the general concept to be remembered in the center circle. Some reasons for keeping your bedroom clean are written in smaller circles, which branch out from the main concept. The number of "branches" off the main concept will vary depending upon the topic.

Photos

Remembering why they need to do certain tasks can be confusing for some children and adults with autism. One solution is to take before and after photographs depicting different situations. To illustrate why you brush your hair, take a photograph of a person with messy, unkempt hair and a second photograph of the same person with a well-groomed hairstyle. You can make your own photos with a digital camera and have the student and her peers "act" out the scenarios. Or similar items can be purchased through educational companies that offer language materials. See the Resource Guide for a list of suggested suppliers.

How????

Do you know a student with autism who forgets how to make her favorite meal, retrieve email messages, or set the table? If a student has problems remembering how to complete some tasks, these strategies can be helpful.

Checklist

Write out instructions for the completion of activities. The written instructions can be paired with a photograph or simple drawing. Consider laminating the page so each step can be crossed or checked off as it is completed. The instruction pages can be wiped clean and placed in a binder for future use. Longer tasks with many steps such as making coffee are easy to complete using this strategy. (See Figures 4.23 to 4.25.)

Fig. 4.23

1.

2.

3.

4.

5.

6.

Fig. 4.24

1. filter

2. 4 scoops coffee

3. put in machine

4. coffee pot

5. water

6. pour in

Fig. 4.25

1. Put filter in basket.

2. Place 4 scoops of coffee into filter.

3. Place filter basket into machine.

4. Place coffee pot on burner.

5. Fill pitcher with water.

6. Pour water into machine.

Finished–coffee will be ready to serve in 5 minutes.

A checklist can be created for any task. Some skills may have many complicated steps that are difficult to remember. Checklists can include icons or pictures as an added cue. The student can follow the steps in the checklist to complete tasks such as using the computer, making a sandwich, or remembering how to program the VCR. See Figure 4.26.

Some people with autism spectrum disorders may be overwhelmed by a lot of information on a page. For them, it is helpful to put the individual steps that they need to do on separate cards. They can follow the steps on one card, then physically move it (into a box or on a key ring) and progress through the sequence.

Fig. 4.26

How to Search the Internet	
Turn the computer on.	
Double click on the Internet Explorer Icon to open it.	
Click on the box labeled "Search."	
Type the word or phrase for what you are looking for.	
Click on GO.	

Memory Plan

A memory plan is an advanced tool for students who are included in general education. A memory plan is useful when preparing to study for a test or a quiz. To use a memory plan, the student must determine:

- what is important,
- how to paraphrase the information she needs to remember,
- the strategy she will use to help remember it, and
- when and how she will be tested on the information.

Some students with autism may need adult help to complete the plan. The student might fill out the plan with the adult, with the adult prompting her with the information. (For example, tell the student to study pages 110 and 111 in the social studies textbook and also review the worksheet titled "The Road to War.") The adult could also complete the plan for the student. See Figure 4.27 on the next page.

Fig. 4.27

Name: _____ Class: _____ Date: _____

Material to be Remembered

Ideas: _____ Facts: _____ How to do things: _____

Topic or Subject Matter

_____

Information Sources

Book: _____ Notes: _____ Other sources: _____

_____

Ways of Condensing Material

Diagrams: _____ Underline/Highlight: _____ Key Words List: _____

Written Summary: _____ On computer: _____ On audio tape: _____

Registration in Memory (Best time of day, duration of work, amount of break time)

Time Needed: _____ Best hours for registration: _____

Breaks: _____

Self Testing (What time and with whom)

Times: _____ Alone: _____ With a family member: _____

With a Friend: _____

(Adapted from Levine, Mel, *Educational Care*, Cambridge, MA: Educators Publishing Service, 1994.)

Temporal Sequential Skills

Michael, a student with autism who had a long-standing history of aggression, presented us with a multitude of challenges. He was placed in our program, which was developed for adolescents with autism and severe behavior challenges. The first day Michael attended the program, the staff counted 95 aggressive incidents. Non-contingent reinforcement (reinforcement provided randomly throughout the day) of favorite food items was used on the second day to enrich Michael's educational environment. In other words, the reinforcement was not related to whether he did or did not do any particular behavior (rewards did not need to be earned). The program was extremely successful and the staff prepared to work toward making reinforcement contingent upon absence of aggression. This meant that they would not provide a reward until after Michael refrained from aggressive behavior for a specified time period (e.g., 15 minutes).

What seemed like a natural progression brought on increased aggression. Initially, it seemed possible that Michael was not willing to wait for reinforcement and that he would just have to learn to wait. However, the simple visual cue of placing a picture of the reinforcement (Skittles, Oreos, Goldfish, Pepsi) cut into three parts on his wall was enough for him to understand that the reinforcement was available and that he was gradually working towards his goal. Michael was able to wait all along. He just wanted assurance that we would honor our promise of future reinforcement.

Michael's rate of aggression declined from an average of 87 occurrences (6 of which were severe, causing injury to staff) during the first month to 12 per month at present (none of which resulted in staff injury). Time intervals were started at 3 five-minute intervals and moved to 3 fifteen-minute intervals. This occurred over the course of two years. The results are a powerful indicator that visual supports can increase understanding, alleviate frustration, and make a dramatic impact on behavior.

We live in a world of sequence and order. Days, months, and years all follow a predictable sequence, and so do many of our activities. On average, we don't go to school on a Saturday, we don't eat breakfast at night, and we don't place the spaghetti sauce into a pot of boiling spaghetti. In order to participate in life as independently and efficiently as possible, we need a basic understanding of temporal sequential skills—an understanding of task order and time concepts.

So, you might wonder what kinds of tasks require the use of temporal sequential skills. They cover a wide range of tasks (simple to complex) including, but not limited to:

- Understanding time of day (morning/afternoon/night)
- Telling time
- Calendar use
- Following a schedule
- Understanding that gratification (reinforcement) will be delayed (see Chapter 7 for more on reinforcement)
- Following a sequence (brushing teeth, using a computer, completing a math problem, using a calendar, following a story)
- Following a schedule
- Reading using left to right and top to bottom progression
- Relating past experiences
- Number sequence and sequencing math problems
- Letter formation sequence for handwriting and left to right progression for writing words, sentences, and paragraphs
- Understanding historical perspective
- Sequencing homework activities

People with ASD of all ages may experience many difficulties in this area. As we all know, confusion can often lead to problematic behavior, so detecting difficulties with temporal sequential skills can help prevent challenging behavior. One way to determine whether someone is having problems in this area would be to look at the kinds of skills that are not progressing or that lead to problematic behavior. If these deficits relate to the skills listed above, difficulties in temporal sequential functioning may exist. You may also know that temporal sequential skills are a problem because the student with autism has not yet been formally taught these concepts or because you have been unsuccessful in teaching these skills. Some of the signs that a learner is having difficulty with temporal sequential skills may be:

- He asks repeated questions about the events of the day or the occurrence of favorite activities.
- He may have significant difficulty understanding the concept of later or wait (and may present behavioral challenges as a result).
- When performing a multi-step task, he may not perform the steps in sequence and needs constant reminders of what comes next (e.g., he may forget to put on underwear before putting on pants, brushes teeth before putting toothpaste on the toothbrush, points to the picture of the school bus on a picture schedule or signs "home" at the beginning of the day, cannot sequence numbers or pictures).

Children and adults with autism spectrum disorders have varied capabilities and needs. Some have other challenges such as cognitive impairment, motor impairment, or other learning disabilities that require that visual strategies be individualized (for instance, by breaking instructions into smaller steps, making a support larger, using adaptive devices, or teaching a prerequisite skill before teaching the more complex skill). Others may have average or above average intelligence and may be able to learn to use visual strategies with a simple explanation, a written reminder, or a model. As always, when approaching something new with a student with autism, reinforcement is critical. A moment-to-moment assessment of what the learner is interested in is key to successful instruction.

VISUALIZE THIS: IDEAS, IDEAS, IDEAS

Time Concepts

How many times during the day do you glance at your watch or at the clock on your dashboard to see the time? Our days revolve around the clock. Timepieces tell us that we have fifteen minutes more to sleep, that we are late for a meeting with our boss, or that we have five minutes left to finish our presentation. Without the use of timepieces, our days would have little or no structure, making it difficult for us to transition from one activity to the next. Unless you are able to determine the passage of time or the time of day by using the sun, then using a watch will be the most efficient method for you.

Children with ASD must understand basic number concepts (number identification, counting, one-to-one correspondence) before being introduced to time concepts. The general concept of time is abstract and some students will have difficulty with this skill.

Visual Representations of the Passage of Time

Many students with ASD have difficulty understanding the passage of time. They do not understand the difference between one minute, five hours, or two days. As a result, they can become frustrated or anxious waiting for a specific event to occur, or may not be able to pace themselves when completing a task that needs to be done by a certain time. It can be helpful to provide these students with visual representations of the passage of time.

Timers

Timepieces, whether in the form of a watch, clock, or timer, provide visual representation. If a student needs to finish a task in a certain amount of time (reading assignments, tests, or group activities) the use of a common kitchen timer, an hourglass, or a visual timer will indicate how much time is left before the interval will be finished.

A visual timer shows elapsed time by using a colored wheel that decreases in size as time passes. This eliminates the need for the student to understand how to read a traditional clock face and shows how much time is left in an interval. Another type of visual timer called a Time Tracker™ gives a color-coded visual cue as to the amount of time remaining to complete a task (the green lighted section means there is plenty of time, yellow means time is running short, and red means time is almost up). The user can program the amount of time that the different sections stay lit. See references at the end of the chapter to see where to purchase these items.

Some timers are available which give the option of setting a warning signal a minute or two before the timer rings. (See references for more information.) Using any of these devices will help students understand when an interval begins and when it will be finished. You can find photos of these three types of timers in the color insert. (See Figures 5.1a, 5.1b, 5.1c in the color insert.)

Photographs

As illustrated in the opening case story, photographs can be used to help a student gauge the amount of time left until he receives a reward. To use this strategy, take photographs of the different types of reinforcements available to the student. Then, cut the pictures into two or more pieces. The student will earn one piece of the puzzle each time he achieves his objective, gradually working towards the final goal. This visual cue shows that reinforcement is available (Figures 5.2 and 5.3).

See Chapter 7 (Motivation) for additional examples of visual teaching strategies that can be used to help individuals with autism delay gratification.

Besides using photos to help children with ASD wait for reinforcement, you can also use photographs to give them a sense of how much longer it will be until an anticipated event occurs. For example, if your child is waiting for a trip to the beach, give him

Fig. 5.2

Fig. 5.3

one piece of a beach photograph every day until the picture is complete and it is time to leave for vacation. Or, if he is waiting for his father to come home from a trip, give him one piece of a photo of his father every day until the day he is expected home.

An alternate solution to visually represent an event that may happen within the next few weeks or months is to show the student a jar full of marbles. Tell him that when the jar is empty, it will be the day of the event. Then, each day, remove one marble until the jar is empty, indicating the day of the event.

Calendars

Daily, monthly, or weekly calendars can show the passage of time to students who have difficulty understanding when activities or events will occur. You can use written words, photographs, pictorial representations, or a combination to represent activities such as going to the zoo, the barber, or a birthday party. Children can mark off the days that have passed (see Figure 5.4). When a student first be-

Fig. 5.4

FEBRUARY						
Sunday	Monday	Tuesday	Wednesday	Thursday	Friday	Saturday
						1 Party
2 *Special Event* Visit Grandma	3	4	5 Class trip to museum	6	7	8
9	10	11 DOCTOR	12	13	14 Valentine's Party!	15
16 Game	17 SCHOOL CLOSED	18	19	20	21	22 Haircut
23	24	25 Dentist	26	27 Shopping	28	

gins to use this method, start with a daily calendar and have him remove a page at the end of the school day. Begin with a simple calendar and individualize it as the student makes progress and begins to understand the passage of time.

Time of Day

One idea to help children understand the time of day (morning, afternoon, and night) is to set up a schedule with photographs that represent those periods of time. Take photographs of the child engaged in specific activities that only occur in the morning, afternoon, and evening. For example, a morning photograph may show him at the kitchen table with breakfast items; an afternoon photograph may show him during recess on the school playground; and an evening photograph might show him preparing for bedtime. Have these photographs available while the child is engaged in these activities in order to help him connect the actual time of day with each activity. ("We eat breakfast in the morning.")

For a child who already can connect activities with a time of day, have him sequence the photos in the order these activities are completed. For example, morning consists of waking up (first in sequence), afternoon involves a school activity (second in sequence), and evening depicts preparing for bed (last in sequence). It is important for the child to be in the photographs. Using a digital or instant Polaroid camera will be the most efficient way to keep the photographs up to date.

Telling Time

Telling time is a difficult concept, even for a typically developing child. In order to be ready to learn time telling, the child should already have an understanding of the passage of time (as described above). Since children with ASD learn best by concrete example, it is best to initially spend some time pairing the time of day on a clock with actual activities occurring during that time. This could be included on a picture schedule if one is already in use. For example, point to the clock at the start of lunch and say, "It's 12 o'clock and time for lunch." Highlight salient features such as where the hour and minute hand are positioned.

Start time telling instruction after this pairing has been initiated. Since telling time to the hour is the easiest to learn, start with this skill first. You may want to color code the hour and minute hand so it is initially easier to differentiate the hands. The colors can be systematically faded (refer to fading procedures in Chapter 9).

After the student learns to tell time to the hour, introduce time to the half hour, then time to the quarter hour, then by five-minute intervals, and finally by one-minute intervals. Use colors, arrows, or other visual cues to highlight the feature/time interval you are focusing on. There are many teaching clocks available commercially to help with this process. They can be found in most educational catalogs or retail stores. Once the child has mastered telling time on the practice clock, begin pairing the practice clock with the real clock until the child can tell time using a variety of analog clocks.

At the beginning of Chapter 9, there is an example of how to transfer telling time on an analog clock to telling time on a digital clock. For all time telling activities, the student must first have mastered the underlying number concepts used in telling time (e.g., counting by fives, identifying numbers 1-60, etc.).

Organization and Scheduling

Many children and adults with autism do not have an understanding of how the day is structured. Changes in task, from room to room, from one staff member to another, from school to home, and from home to school may be frightening if you are not prepared for the transition.

Schedules can help to reduce stress related to transitions. They provide order and help in sequencing daily events. Schedules can be set up using written words, pictures, or a combination of the two.

Graphic Organizers

Graphic organizers can be used to help a learner to express past experiences. Begin by finding or taking pictures of activities or events that the student has participated in, making sure that he is in the photograph. Then set up the organizer in a timeline fashion (weekly or monthly) to depict past events. Label the months above the photographs and arrange them in sequential order (top to bottom or left to right progression). As previously suggested, use a digital or Polaroid instant camera to keep the organizer up to date with current photographs. This same idea can be used to clarify the concepts of today and yesterday.

Written and Picture Schedules

Fig. 5.5

Many of us cannot get through a day without referring to our date book. They help keep us on schedule and organized. Written and picture schedules are popular options for people with ASD too. There are a multitude of choices available for learners of different abilities. Some students carry a small book with their daily activities recorded in written or pictorial representation inside; for others, a larger classroom-sized schedule is also a possibility. Pictures of activities can be removed or pages can be flipped as each task/activity is completed. For example, Figure 5.5 shows an activity schedule in which "John's" morning activities (writing his name on his paper, clerical filing, etc.) are represented sequentially with photos, one per page.

In their book, *Activity Schedules for Children with Autism* (1999), Drs. Lynn Mc-Clannahan and Patricia Krantz explore activity schedules and how they can be used to increase independence. Please refer to Chapter 2 for an overview of using activity schedules and to their book for a detailed description.

Checklists

Consider using a checklist for any sequential procedure the individual is expected to follow. He can complete items on the checklist and cross them off as they are completed. You can refer to Chapter 2 for other options to indicate task completion. Checklists can be in written form, with pictorial representations, or a combination, depending on the skill of the user. For the beginner, start with one task that he can complete independently. When he can use the checklist correctly, gradually increase the number of items on the list. See Figures 5.6 and 5.7 for two different examples of a Chores Checklist.

Palm Pilots or PDAs

A Palm Pilot™ or personal digital assistant (PDA) can be a valuable tool in helping a student remember when something needs to be done (homework assignments) or when an activity will occur (a family vacation). Using a Palm Pilot™ may

Fig. 5.6

Chores	Finished

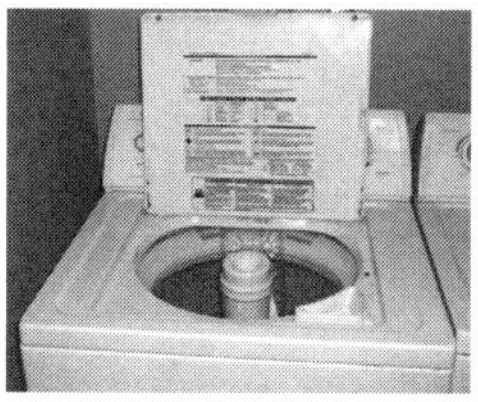	

Fig. 5.7

Chores	Finished
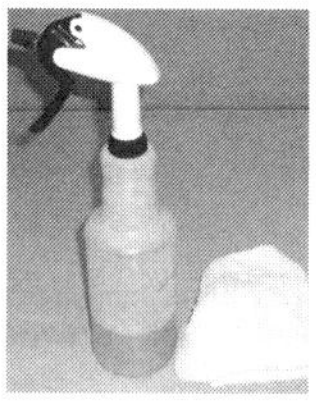 **wash table**	
 **laundry**	
 **empty dishwasher**	
 **set table**	

be challenging for some people with autism, but those with good computer ability or technical skills will benefit from this type of technology. Individuals who need a more concrete representation can use a written calendar instead.

Pill Organizers

Pill organizers can be used to indicate when medication should be taken. Medication organizers come in different styles. Some organizers have the day of the week printed on top, while other more elaborate models can be programmed to set off an alarm. If the person must take medication several times a day, purchase a smaller organizer and place labels on the lid of each compartment to indicate the time the medication should be taken. If the person has trouble telling time, you could also put small symbols on the lids to indicate the time to take each pill. For example, use a picture of a bed to indicate that the medication should be taken at bedtime.

Multi-Step Tasks

People with temporal difficulties have problems sequencing multi-step tasks. They often lose track of what comes next in a long string of skills. Some of these difficulties are linked to problems related to attention and memory and are discussed as separate learning challenges in Chapters 6 and 3, respectively. Strategies below are useful for problems due mostly to sequencing difficulties.

Power Cards™

As described in previous chapters, "the Power Cards™ Strategy is a visual aid that incorporates the child's special interest in teaching him appropriate social interactions including routines, behavior expectations, the meaning of language" (Gagnon). Power Cards can help children with ASD organize a sequence of events or skills. For example, the steps of a task can be written out to help increase the student's independence. Power Cards can be made into small booklets, a single page, or small pocket-sized cards. Learners can keep the card in their pocket for future reference. See the references at the end of the chapter for more information about Power Cards (Figure 5.8).

Fig. 5.8

Dr. Taft knows that dirty hands carry many germs. Germs contain diseases that can make people sick. Dr. Taft always washes his hands before he examines any of his patients.

After you use the bathroom, wash your hands.

1. Turn on the water.
2. Get your hands wet.
3. Put soap on your hands.
4. Rub your hands together to lather.
5. Rinse the soap off your hands.
6. Dry your hands with a paper towel.
7. Throw the paper towel in the garbage.

Photograph/Picture Series

Photographs can be organized to show the sequence of multi-step tasks. For example, if you wanted to teach a child how to set the table, you could take photographs depicting each step for completing the task.

The photographs can be arranged in left to right progression or from top to bottom. The user can keep track of the steps completed in several ways.

1. The photographs can be numbered and the student can follow the numerical sequence.
2. Laminate the photo board and have the student use a dry erase pen or china marker to cross off each step as it is completed. The boards can be wiped off after each use.
3. Use Velcro™ on the back of the photographs and have the student remove the photographs and put them to the side, in a basket, or in a waistband pouch as each step is completed.
4. The student can use his finger to follow along with the sequence.
5. Place a piece of Velcro™ under each picture. An arrow can be moved after each step of the sequence is completed.

See Figures 5.9, 5.10, and 5.11 for examples.

Fig. 5.9

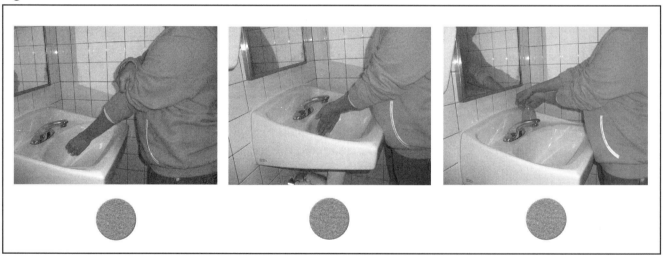

Fig. 5.10

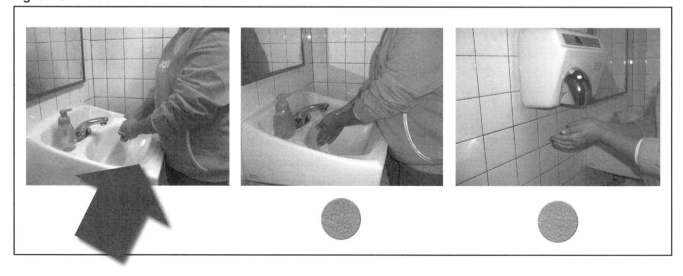

Fig. 5.11

You can also use photographs or pictures to show each step needed to complete a recipe. (See Figure 5.12 on the next page.) These pictures can be arranged in chronological order on a board or placed in a recipe book. Each step can be numbered and the learner can follow the numerical sequence for any recipe.

Maps and Floor Plans

School: Some students are required to make multiple classroom changes throughout the school day. If finding his way from class to class is difficult for a particular child, first make sure hallways throughout the building are visually marked so that one can be distinguished from the other. For example, hallways can be coded with colored tape on the walls. Often times, hallways in larger schools use numbers or letters to name the hall or wing.

Next, make a floor plan of the school and color-code it to correspond with the student's class schedule (e.g., science class, period 1, is green and located in the green hallway). Draw arrows to demonstrate the sequence of transitions from class to class. This will make transitions easier and faster. For example, Figures 5.13, 5.14, and 5.15 (color insert) illustrate three separate maps indicating the path between classes. These can be coordinated following the suggestion of using color codes for books and folders by subject (Chapter 4).

Grocery Store: Going to a grocery store can be overwhelming for some people with autism spectrum disorders. It may be difficult for them to navigate their way through the store. Create a floor plan that coordinates with your local grocery store. Use this floor plan to help individuals find items on their grocery lists faster and more efficiently, by progressing systematically from one end of the store to the other. Use photographs of the items or written words and highlight with colors that coordinate to the aisle the item can be found in. For example, if spaghetti is found in aisle 4, you might glue a photo of a spaghetti box to a green background and color-code aisle 4 green on the floor plan. This will make grocery shopping more efficient and will eliminate needlessly searching for items. (See Figures 5.16 and 5.17 in the color insert.)

Note: As with teaching any new concept using visual or other strategies, it is important to recognize

Fig. 5.12

MAKING MUFFINS

① Preheat Oven 400°

② Get: Muffin mix , 1 egg, ⅓ cup milk, butter, bowl, muffin pan, spoon

③ Open mix   Pour in bowl

④ Add egg, milk, butter

⑤ Mix until lumps are gone

⑥ Pour in muffin pan

Bake for 15 minutes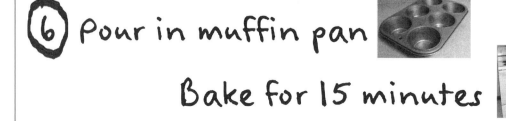

that you need to make learning the new task worthwhile. Therefore, determining what the individual wants and having it readily available to provide reinforcement will be critical for this as well as all new tasks.

Understanding Historical Perspective

Students with ASD who are ready to learn academic material through the use of textbooks may be exposed to content area of history. Typically, these students will have already mastered some time concepts and calendar skills.

We can all probably recall how difficult it was to organize all of the dates and the respective events associated with them as we were studying for a history test. Because language is an area of difficulty for people with autism, pulling out those dates and organizing them into a meaningful sequence can be especially overwhelming. Helping the student do this—by highlighting each date in the chapter and placing the dates and events in sequence on a timeline—can be very useful.

Graphic Organizers and Timelines

Graphic organizers can be valuable tools in helping students with ASD make sense of historical events. We recommend using two different types of graphic organizers at once.

First, we use a basic organizer to gather together the major points, including the date, that the student needs to learn. Place the main event and date in the center circle, with related information (who was involved, where the event occurred, etc.) as offshoots from the main idea.

Next, we create a timeline that shows the date of that event and other related events. Write short descriptive labels for each event depicted (include dates, names, or other pertinent information) and arrange in order. The timeline will give the learner a visual cue that will help him remember the chronological order. Small icons or pictures can also be added as an extra cue. (See Figure 5.18.)

With both of these strategies in place (timeline and graphic organizer) the student has a condensed version of the information in the book which could be used to study the sequence of events in time as well as other related information.

Note: Using a larger size paper or using landscape paper orientation can allow you to add short notes under each period to denote some of the major facts about that era.

Fig. 5.18

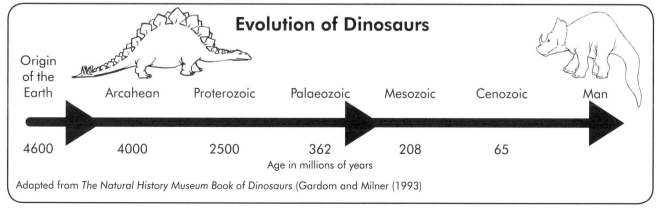

Adapted from *The Natural History Museum Book of Dinosaurs* (Gardom and Milner (1993)

◼ Math Skills

There are many prerequisites to performing math skills such as visual discrimination, symbolic representation (understanding that a symbol represents a number or quantity), and one-to-one correspondence. Math can be abstract, requiring good cognitive functioning. Some students with ASD may do well with number identification and counting, but stop progressing at this point. Others may be able to learn money values, simple computations, and calculator use. Still others may be able to learn advanced math skills such as banking skills, geometry, and algebra. It is important that you have an understanding of the progression of math skill development in order to assess the appropriate sequence of skill instruction for any given student. There are many inexpensive resources/workbooks that grade math skill development and can be purchased at local bookstores or stores that sell educational supplies.

Students who have deficits in sequential skills may experience difficulties completing mathematical problems. They may become confused with multi-step problems or have trouble following the steps necessary to solve equations. Some students may never develop the ability to perform abstract math problems without the use of concrete materials. Still, relying on these types of supports allows them to be involved in academic skills and to learn skills that will increase their independence as adults.

Fig. 5.19

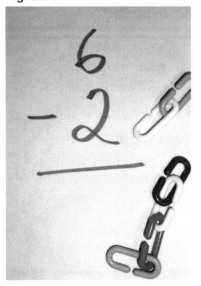

Manipulatives

Manipulatives are widely used to help all young students grasp new math concepts. For students with autism, manipulatives may be useful for a longer period of time, or for explaining concepts that other students may grasp without the use of manipulatives. Refer to Chapters 1 and 2 for considerations when using manipulatives.

Using manipulatives or concrete objects (blocks, poker chips, coins, or beads) helps learners to visualize mathematical problems and give them logical order. For example, Figure 5.19 shows how plastic links can be used for teaching simple addition and subtraction. As the student becomes more successful in completing problems, fade out the use of the manipulatives and slowly introduce the abstract form. As an intermediate step, you might teach the student to use hash marks or dots on the paper in place of the manipulative object. Refer to Chapter 9 for more information on fading visual supports.

Number Lines

Number lines or abacuses can also be used to help students with autism complete mathematical problems. There are a variety of ways to construct a number line. Most commonly, the numbers are arranged horizontally from left to right. If teaching addition, place an arrow with a plus sign above the number line to show that adding is accomplished by moving from the left to the right (increasing numbers). Alternately, for subtraction, an arrow with a minus sign should point to the left (reversing the addition process by decreasing number value). Other cues can be added to make learning easier (e.g., colors, symbols, etc.).

To help the student keep track of how many numbers he has moved to the left or right, you can laminate the number line. Then he can use a dry erase marker and physically mark his jumps. For example, for 5 + 3 he would start with his marker on the five, then count "one" as he draws a jump in the shape of an upside down "U" between the 5 and the 6, "two" as he jumps from 6 to 7, etc.

Graphic Columns

Some students have difficulty keeping numbers lined up correctly when completing written math problems. This can be resolved by using a piece of graph paper or lined paper turned sideways when working on mathematical equations. The learner can easily see the columns; making addition, subtraction, or multiplication problems easier to line up (Figure 5.20).

Fig. 5.20

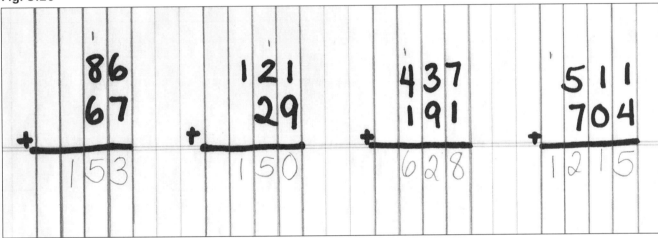

Written Models

Providing students with written examples of completed multi-step math problems allows them to refer back to the mathematical process needed to complete different equations. These sample problems can be placed in a small notebook or on a piece of paper that is attached to the front page of the student's math notebook. The notebook can be organized into different sections based upon which mathematical operation is used (addition, addition with regrouping, multiplication, etc.). The classroom teacher can place a heading on the worksheets to indicate what type of operation is needed to complete the work. Eventually, it would be desirable for the student to be able to complete varied types of mathematical computations on one worksheet page.

Highlighting Important Words

Word problems present students with the challenge of identifying which information is needed to solve the problem and what irrelevant facts can be disregarded. Key words or numbers can be highlighted to help the learner locate important information needed to solve the problem. For example, words or phrases can be underlined, highlighted with color, or typed in a bold font or in a font style that is different from the rest of the problem. The student can then refer to a chart that lists "key" words and the mathematical operation associated with them (Figure 5.21).

It is important to note that this type of list is useful only when the student understands the process of the computation included in the math problem. For example, a student would already have to know how to add before moving to an addition word problem. Also, the teacher must be careful at first not to present word problems where key words appear but indicate a different operation than listed in the chart (for example, problems with the words "how many more than" sometimes require subtraction, rather than addition to solve). The key words in the example below are suggested terms that can be found in this type of problem. Use the curriculum as a guide and adapt it to include the terms in the curriculum series the student is using in school.

Fig. 5.21

Addition	Subtraction	Multiplication	Division	Equals
Increased by	Decreased by	Of times	Per	Is
More than	Minus	Multiplied by	Ratio of	Are
Combined	Difference	Increased/	Quotient of	Was
Together	Less than	decreased by a	Percent	Were
Total of	Fewer than	factor of		Will be
Sum				Gives
Added to				Yields

Adapted from: www.iss.stthomas.edu/studyguides/mathproblems

Graphic Organizers

Using graphic organizers will give logical order to multi-step problems. For example, Figure 5.22 shows how a graphic organizer can help a student visualize how multiplication problems are solved. You can also use concrete objects (such as blocks, beads, coins) with this type of strategy, and as previously suggested move to more abstract forms, such as hash marks or dots (see Figure 5.23).

Some students may only need to refer to an example of a completed graphic organizer in order to solve an equation. Others may need to create a graphic organizer for each problem. If this is necessary, a small dry erase board can make this process simpler for the student.

Number Cards

Addition with carrying (regrouping) is challenging for many children who cannot understand where to place the numerals. It requires the understanding of place value. Number cards can help students learn how to correctly place numbers in the ones and tens columns before they completely understand place value.

Before using this strategy, first prepare the number cards. Cut out 10 each of two different shapes—for example, 10 small circles and 10 small triangles. For a stronger visual cue, use a different color of paper for each set. Write the numerals 0 to 9 on each set of shapes. Designate one set of shapes as being for the "ones" and the other set as

Fig. 5.22

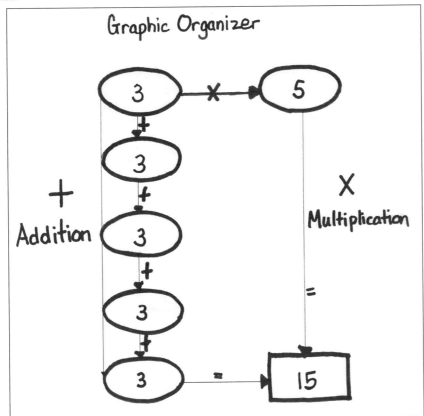

Fig. 5.23

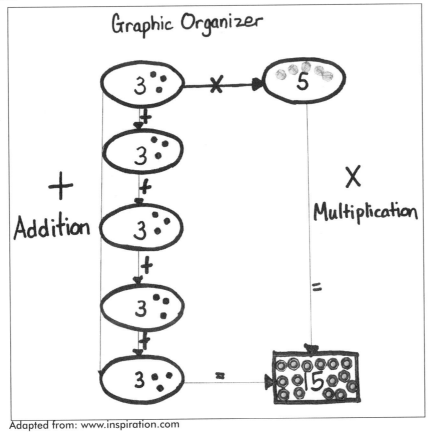

Adapted from: www.inspiration.com

Fig. 5.24

Fig. 5.25

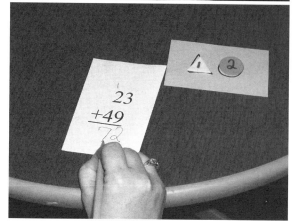

being for the "tens." (Figure 5.24 shows circles being used for the ones and triangles for the tens.) Next, prepare the answer card by tracing around one of your "tens" shapes and one of your "ones" shapes on an index card. (For example, draw a triangle followed by a circle, if you are using triangles for the "tens" and "circles" for the ones.)

Next, give the student a two-digit addition problem and have him perform the addition of the "ones column first." Using the number cards, have him place this total onto the answer card. Make sure he uses the proper number cards for the ones and tens. These shapes serve as a visual cue as to where the "ones" should be placed and how to "carry" the "tens" numerals.

Next, have the student transfer the number card in the ones place from the answer card to the written problem, placing it in the ones position. Then have him move the number card in the tens place from the answer card to the written problem and add up the tens column.

In the pictures on page 78, the student is completing the problem 49 + 23. He is instructed to solve the simple addition problem 3 + 9 (adding the "ones") separately. He then uses the removable numbered shapes and places the "ones" (2) in the correct position and carries the "tens" (1) above the tens column. The shape cues can be faded until the student demonstrates mastery without cues (Figures 5.24 and 5.25).

▓ Reading

Reading is a secondary language system. Our primary language system is words, which are used to symbolize actual objects or concepts. Written language is a symbol of the spoken word. The process of reading is complex unless you have a clear understanding of the order in which these words need to be arranged. For example, if a student is matching the pictures held in his hand with the ones laid out on the table, it would not matter which picture was matched first or last. In reading, a student must start on the left and move to the right, following a set sequence. Here are some ways to highlight that sequence for students with ASD.

Colored Dots

Use colored dots (green and red) to indicate where to begin reading and where to finish. This helps the child to remember to read in a left to right progression. Additionally, when he is required to read a smaller portion of a chapter or passage, the colored dots will make it clear to him what is the required reading.

Numbering Text

If a textbook is laden with photographs, graphics, and text, some students have difficulty determining what part of the page to read first. Before asking a student to read a complicated page in a textbook, systematically teach him to read less complex pages. We recommend following this sequence:

1. One sentence on a page,
2. One paragraph on a page,
3. Two paragraphs on a page,
4. One full page of text,
5. One full page with two columns.

Use a colored dot to indicate where to begin reading. When a page has columns, place a green dot with a number 1 on top of the first column and a green dot with a number 2 on top of the second column. When pictures, graphs, or tables are on a page, place numbered stickers over each item so the student will understand what order to read each area of the page.

As an alternative to the above method, you can photocopy parts of a book and then cut and paste the sections in the order they should be read. Also, if a text contains too many distractions on a page, you can photocopy the pages, remove the distracting material, and glue or paste the segments on another piece of paper in the order the student should read them.

Keeping Place with a Ruler

To help a child keep his place when reading large sections of text, have him use a ruler, slide, or a strip of paper to keep his place on the page. Rulers may be too long and inflexible for following along in a book with relatively narrow pages. In this case, strips of paper or poster board may need to be custom cut to match the width of the text.

Graphic Organizers

Graphic organizers can also be used to illustrate important information and to put the sequence of events in correct order. The student can fill out the graphic organizer as he is reading a story. He can then refer back to the information he has gathered. (See Figure 5.26.) You can make graphic organizers more fun to use by drawing them in interesting shapes. (See Figure 5.27.)

Fig. 5.26

EVENTS	
What happened?	
When did this occur?	
Where did it happen?	
How did this happen?	
Who was involved?	
Why did it occur?	

■ Writing

According to Janet Lerner, a learning disabilities expert, "the process of handwriting is intricate and depends on many different skills and abilities. Writing requires accurate perception of the graphic symbol patterns." Writing may be even more difficult for children with ASD, who may have fine motor delays, problems

Fig. 5.27

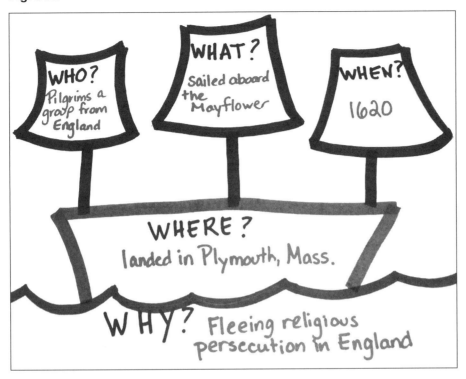

with visual-motor integration, or difficulty remembering the sequence of strokes. Below are several visual strategies to help a student with this process. Other strategies to help with writing are included in Chapter 4.

Visual Strategies for Forming Letters (Handwriting Mechanics)

This strategy is useful for students who can write but have poor letter formation or difficulty remembering the starting point for writing individual letters. The starting point for the formation of letters (manuscript or cursive) can be highlighted with a green star or another icon (see Figure 5.28). Also, each stroke in the formation of the letter can be numbered (see Figure 5.29 on the next page). The numbered steps can have written directions associated with the letter formation for the learner to use as a reference. (Adapted from *Creative Cursive Workbook*, 2001.) Letter cards illustrating the steps in letter formation can be posted in the classroom or smaller versions can be placed inside students' notebooks or on their desks (Figure 5.30).

Fig. 5.28

Fig. 5.29

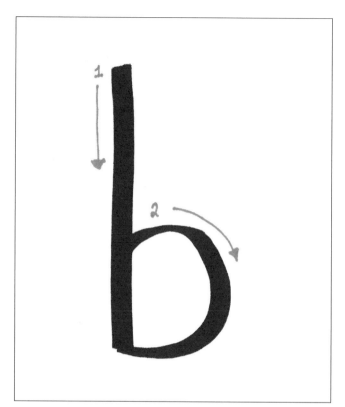

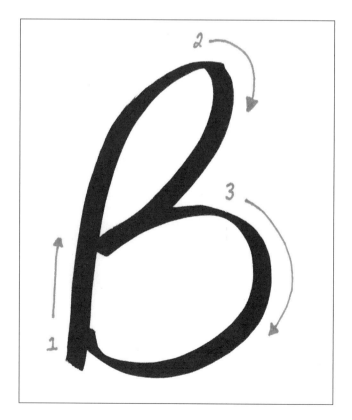

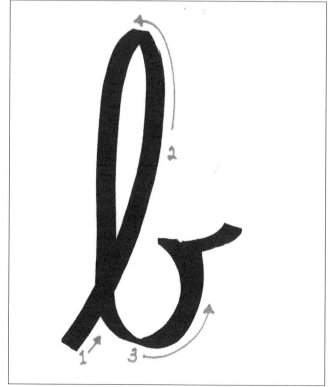

Fig. 5.30

Adapted from: www.handwritinghelpforkids.com

Graphic Organizers for Written Expression

Use graphic organizers to help a student correctly sequence the parts of a story, business letter, or paragraph. The example shown in Figure 5.31 can help a student ensure that all of the parts of the story are in the correct order.

When first teaching a learner to use this kind of graphic organizer, begin by filling out the graphic organizer for him (with information taken from the child's verbal description). Later, leave blank spaces in the graphic organizer, and have him complete parts of the story himself. As the student is successful at filling in more and more information, provide a completely blank graphic organizer for him to complete.

Fig. 5.31

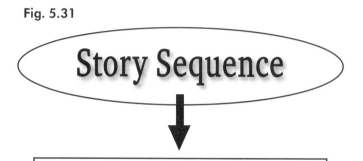

Story Sequence
I went to Great Adventure with my family.
I saw a great big fountain when I got into the park.
We went on the Batman ride and it was fast!
Next we went on Freefall. It was so scary.
We decided to take a break and eat lunch. I had pizza.
It was hot and we had to wait in line for the water rides.
We had a great day!

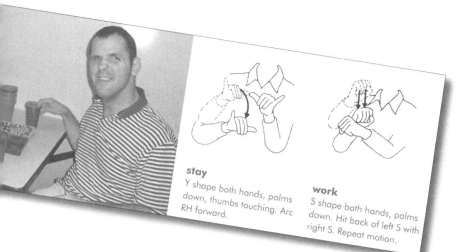

Using Visual Supports to Increase Attending

Ivania, a sixteen-year-old student with Asperger's syndrome, was placed on homebound instruction after threatening staff with scissors. When she entered our program as a full-time student, we performed an initial assessment of her skills. I can remember vividly having my first discussion with her about what she wanted to include in her IEP. Ivania was curled up on her living room couch, wearing nothing but a bed sheet. She made no eye contact, and resisted participation in developing her IEP. After establishing a rapport with her, we began to entertain the idea of focusing on academic goals. We knew that she could perform in some academic areas at a high school level, but without a comprehensive educational evaluation we could only guess about her level of performance.

We approached Ivania's Child Study Team about an educational evaluation. After initially thinking we were crazy (they had not been able to get Ivania to participate in testing previously), the Learning Consultant agreed to meet with her to get an idea of what kind of testing would be most appropriate. Fortunately, Ivania charmed the Learning Consultant and she began to plan an assessment strategy. She decided to administer the WIATT II (Wechsler Individual Achievement Test – 2ⁿᵈ Edition) with the modification of breaking the reading into smaller passages using cue cards with the correct answer written on the back. Reading smaller passages reduced mental fatigue so that the assessment process was less overwhelming for Ivania. Having the answers on the back gave Ivania the correct answer for future reference, which made being incorrect less intimidating.

Test results indicated that Ivania's reading and math reasoning skills were at a college level. The satisfaction that Ivania received as a result of finding concrete evidence of her level of intelligence helped her to develop into a student who could ask questions about her educational program at her IEP meeting. She began to advocate for her own needs, astounding professionals from her district who had witnessed many of her previous failures. There is no greater gift that you can provide an individual than a sense of self-esteem and respect for his or her own capabilities and accomplishments. Simple modifications in the visual presentation of an assessment were all that was needed to help this student achieve that goal.

Often, children and adults with autism have difficulty regulating attention. We all know that it is virtually impossible to gain information and skills when you are having significant difficulties with attending. Even intermittent attention may result in inconsistency in what is learned and how the information is acted upon. According to Dr. Mel Levine (1994), attention problems in general can be related to difficulties in three areas:

- Mental energy (ability to sustain attention long enough to obtain all of the relevant information);
- Processing (attending to information well enough to understand it);
- Production (attending when acting on or responding to information).

We need attention in order to:

- Process sensory stimuli in our environment (sight, sound, smell, touch);
- Keep from responding impulsively while weighing the pros and cons of certain responses;
- Maintain a level of awareness when exposed to important information;
- Avoid dangerous situations (e.g., moving vehicles while crossing a street, pouring hot liquid, taking medication);
- Process all of the information presented, not just part.

We know that students with autism in particular can have problems shifting attention, and, as a result, may pay attention to irrelevant stimuli. They also may be unable to shift their attention from something of interest to something less interesting.

What better way to attract attention than to introduce a visual strategy that highlights what should be attended to, how long to attend, and how to plan through a response? We all have used a variety of visual strategies to enhance our own performances. We mark our calendar so we will pay attention to certain events, we highlight important information that we have read, we keep a diary of the foods we have eaten when we are on a diet in order to see what is necessary to achieve our goal. Why do kids attend so well to video games? Perhaps it is because they are visually interesting. Videotapes of learning material can be enhanced with special effects and animation, which is much more interesting than our typical learning environment. Let's explore some ways that you can increase the attention of your student.

VISUALIZE THIS: IDEAS, IDEAS, IDEAS

Maintaining Mental Energy

According to Mel Levine (1994) mental energy enables us to stay focused long enough to extract the pertinent information. It is "the aspect of brain function that energizes our alertness and enables us to exert mental effort." Some ways to attract and sustain the student's attention are explained below.

Color Codes

This strategy involves using a traffic signal placed on the student's desk as a cue (Figures 6.1 and 6.2 in color insert). The traffic signal is a visual representation of how well a student is attending. The "lights" on the traffic signal represent different levels of attention that are demonstrated by the student.

The visual support in Figure 6.1 is made by attaching colored construction paper circles to a binder ring. These circles can be flipped easily so the teacher can change the light depending on what the child is doing. If the light is red, the child needs to stop what she is doing and listen to the teacher. A yellow light signals caution; if the child's attention is drifting, she needs to refocus. A green light tells the child that she is doing a good job paying attention. The traffic light poster shown in Figure 6.2 can be posted in the classroom if the student needs a reminder of what the different colors mean.

Sign Language

Sign language can be used to prompt students to maintain attention to the teacher and/or the task materials. This reduces the number of verbal prompts used

Fig. 6.3

stay
Y shape both hands, palms down, thumbs touching. Arc RH forward.

work
S shape both hands, palms down. Hit back of left S with right S. Repeat motion.

and decreases the need to repeat directions. It also allows the teacher or aide to prompt the student from any distance.

To make it clear to the learner that she needs to focus her attention, the teacher can sign "stop – look – listen." A card with the sign representing the task ("work") and a photograph of the student engaged in the activity can be used to remind the learner to maintain her attention on her work (Figure 6.3 on the previous page). You can put this card down on the student's desk or table as a reminder. You can also just write the word "work" on it if the student can read (rather than using pictures of the signs). Figures 6.4 and 6.5 show the teacher using the manual sign "sit" while the student performs the action.

Fig. 6.4

Fig. 6.5

Fig. 6.6

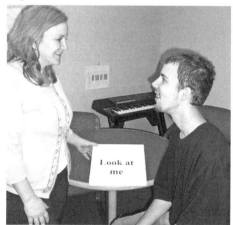

Change Visual Aids

Visual stimuli should be frequently changed to increase attention. If possible, new visuals should be incorporated into the lesson approximately every 45 seconds. This may occur when the teacher moves from one part of the room to another, or when he or she actually changes the manipulative—for example, by writing on the chalkboard, using an overhead, or holding up varied materials.

Cue Cards

If a student has trouble staying focused, the teacher can place a cue card on the student's desk as an indicator that she needs to stay on task. The cue card can have either a pictorial reminder, or a written reminder, as shown in Figure 6.6. The teacher could also pose as the cue by standing near the student as a signal that it is time to "get ready" or be prepared to answer a question.

Color Highlights

Highlight key words or phrases in a textbook or other reading material using bright markers or highlighters. Red or yellow often works best. Important text can also be underlined. Bold fonts can make key information stand out; a larger size font draws the reader's attention. On a blackboard, you can use colored chalks to draw attention. A laser pointer is another useful tool for attracting attention.

Blocking and Framing Passages

Blocking or framing involves highlighting the text by placing a boxed outline around the important or critical sections. This technique can be used to draw attention to information that is presented on a larger field. When blocking or framing, the best color paper to sustain attention is light blue. Put only one idea or concept on the page. Put a frame around key points you want the student to focus on. The easiest way to do this is to use the formatting tools available in your word processing software. You can also manually box text by using a marker or a brightly colored pen.

The chart in Figure 6.7 shows how and why great care should be taken in the layout of written information. People tend to focus most on the information presented at the very top of a page. Then they scan quickly over intervening material until they get to the review and conclusion.

Fig. 6.7

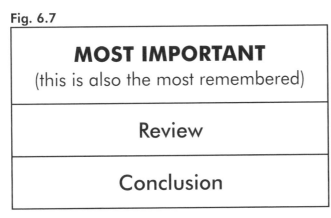

Attending During Processing

Many students with ASD have difficulty maintaining attention while new information is presented. They may have problems with information that is presented orally, visually, or in any other modality. To learn, students must filter out irrelevant stimuli and focus on what is relevant. If they cannot process incoming information effectively, they will most likely have trouble with comprehension and retention. Some ideas on improving attention during the "input" stage are described below.

Icons

Use icons to attract attention to important information. For example, to highlight key points on paper or on the blackboard, use stars, dots, or arrows. Be careful not to use too many icons per page. Sometimes it is useful to use different styles of icons to highlight different types of information (e.g., use stars to highlight important dates and hearts to highlight important vocabulary to learn).

Highlighting

Use colored markers on a white dry erase board or on overheads to draw the student's attention to key points or details that should not be overlooked. Making important facts more salient in a "sea" of irrelevant information will make the learning process easier for students who have difficulty in this area. Figure 6.8 (color insert) shows how highlighting can make the operational sign in a mathematical equation very noticeable.

Fig. 6.9

Written Directions

Mel Levine (1994) believes that students may process information more deeply when it is presented in more than one way. If a student has trouble processing instructions for class work or homework, reinforce verbal instructions by also writing the directions on the blackboard. It may also help to show the student the materials she will need to use to do the homework. Figure 6.9 illustrates how this can be done.

Graphic Organizers

Graphic organizers can help students determine what information is relevant to the lesson. If the essential information is outlined for the students in advance, they will be able to stay focused on the lesson without worrying about what information is important for them to write down. Depending upon the learner's previous experience with graphic organizers, the amount of information completed will vary (Figures 6.10, 6.11, and 6.12). The student must maintain attention and follow through the entire lesson in order to enter the missing information into the graphic organizer. This graphic organizer can be used later as a study guide. Refer to Chapter 2 for more detailed information about using graphic organizers.

Fig. 6.10

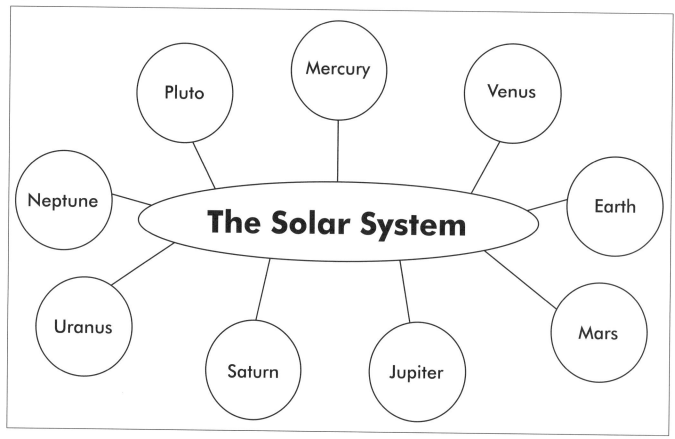

Fig. 6.11

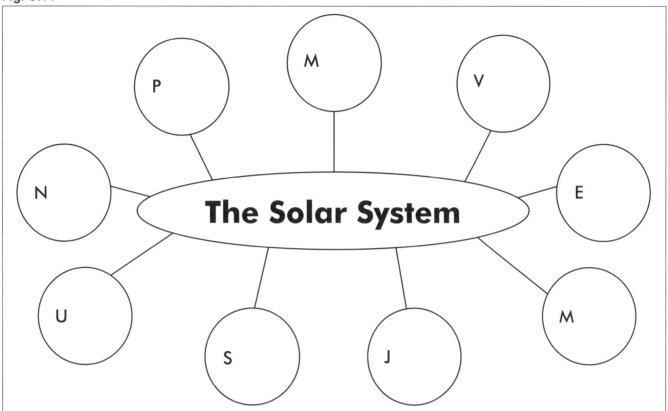

Fig. 6.12

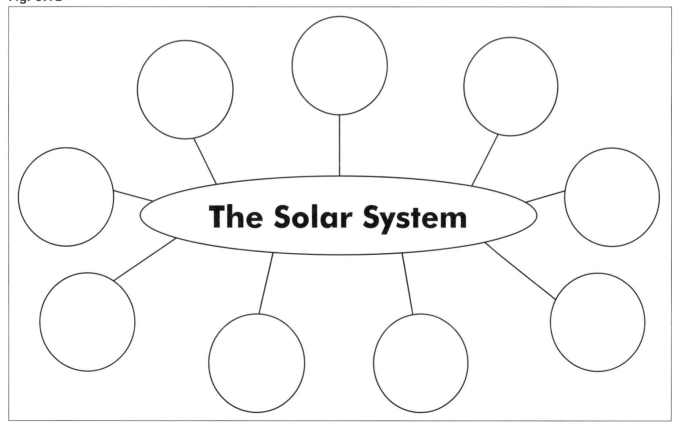

Visual Cues

As stated earlier in this chapter, students with ASD can have difficulty shifting attention. This is particularly true when the shift is from something interesting to something less interesting. Visual cues such as flicking the lights on and off, dimming the lights, or using a strobe light or other flashing light can act as an automatic startle response and signal an upcoming change in activity. The visual cue can be paired with a verbal direction such as "It's time to go back to work."

If a student is disturbed or over-stimulated by flashing lights, try some other kind of visual cue. For example, to cue a change in activities, use a picture of the next activity or an icon that stands for "change activity." You can hold up this picture or post it on the board five minutes before the transition is going to happen.

For young children or those with significant language problems, you could give them something to hold to cue them that change is coming. For example, give a playground ball to the child to carry several minutes before going out for recess, or give her the bottle of liquid soap to carry before the class is taken to visit the restroom.

Finally, activity schedules can serve as a means of letting students know they will need to shift attention. For example, if a student's schedule shows a picture of art class followed by a picture of lunch, she will understand that when she finishes art class it will be time to make the transition to lunch.

■ Attending During Production

If your attention is diverted because of other stimuli around you, you will likely find it difficult to sustain your attention long enough to respond to information. Individuals who have weak production control are easily distracted by their environment and cannot stay on task. The following ideas can help students stay on task and "tuned in" to the activity they are involved in.

Advanced Organizers

To extrapolate important facts from written material, Mel Levine (1994) suggests using an "Advanced organizer." This is merely a list of questions that the student should think about when reading (Figure 6.13). This type of checklist will also improve reading comprehension and help with later recall. Students should be encouraged to write down the answers to questions if they are likely to forget the answers and/or to jot down the page number where the answer is located.

Fig. 6.13

What to Think about When Reading Little House on the Prairie

- Where does Laura live?
- What types of activities does Laura enjoy?
- Who are her siblings?
- What does Laura's father do for a living?
- When does the story take place?

(Adapted from Levine, M., *Educational Care*. Cambridge, MA: Educators Publishing Service, 1994.)

Charts or Tables

Using charts or tables to take a step-by-step approach to planning and carrying out large projects can help students attend to the task. In the examples shown (Figures 6.14-16 on pages 94-96), a learner can see what steps she must accomplish in order to complete her final product, a birdhouse. The addition of pictures will also focus the learner's attention. The student must follow and complete each step before moving on to another part of the project. As the student completes each step, she can cross it off. This type of instructional aid could be placed on index cards that the student would flip over or put in a discard pile or box. The cards could then be used over and over by others who might work on a similar project.

Although the example shown is for a hands-on task, this strategy can also be used for completing a multi-step academic activity, such as writing a book report. For example:

1. Go to the library.
2. Find a book you want to read.
3. Read the book by April 11th (etc.)

Breaking Work Into Smaller Units

Sometimes it is easier for students to stay focused if the task is broken down into smaller units. Perhaps a student is required to complete 25 math problems. If the page is divided into smaller units, the student can go to the teacher after she completes each segment for feedback and then be directed back to work. As the student becomes more proficient at maintaining her attention, the amount of required work can be increased in small increments.

To divide a page into smaller units:

- Draw a colored box around the first 5 problems, then later draw another colored box around the next 5 problems to complete; or
- Cut the page up into separate pieces according to the number of problems you wish the student to complete at a time.

Written Contracts

Having an agreed-upon deadline with a payoff may help some children and adults with ASD stay focused on a project and maintain their attention. Written contracts can be drawn up between the students and the teacher or parent. The contract will clearly state **who** is responsible for doing the work, **what** the task will be, **when** the deadline is for completion, and **how well** the task must be done (Cooper, et al., 1987). In addition, contracts specifically outline what the reward will be when it is fulfilled (Figure 6.17 on page 97).

For the contract to be a visual support, it is important that it be displayed somewhere that the child can see it and be reminded of what she needs to do to earn the chosen reinforcer. Reading skills are necessary for this type of support.

Calendars

Make use of calendars to visually plan out big projects and clearly indicate deadlines. First draw up an outline of what steps need to be completed in order to reach the goal. Then, determine how much time to spend on each aspect and plot

Fig. 6.14

GOAL: Building a Birdhouse

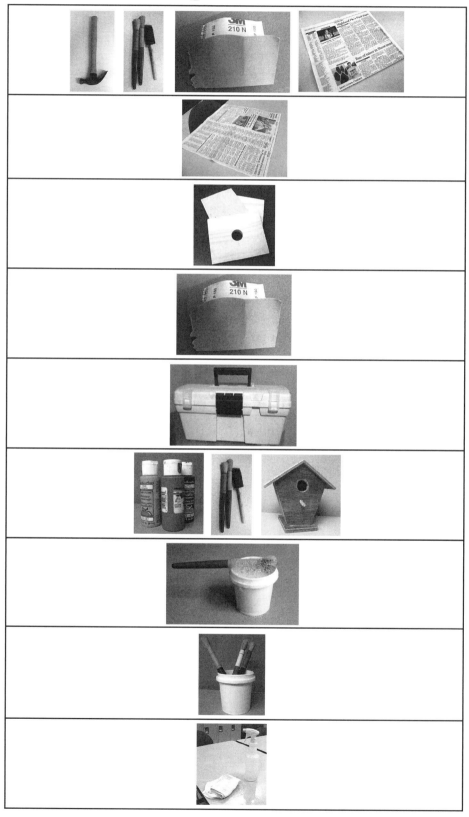

Fig. 6.15

GOAL: Building a Birdhouse

1. Get materials.	
2. Cover table.	
3. Build birdhouse.	
4. Sand wood.	
5. Put tools away.	
6. Paint.	
7. Wash brushes.	
8. Put brushes away.	
9. Clean up.	

Fig. 6.16

GOAL: Building a Birdhouse

1. Collect all tools and supplies needed.	
2. Place newspaper on work area.	
3. Assemble birdhouse (follow directions).	
4. Sand all sides of the birdhouse until smooth.	
5. Put tools away.	
6. Paint birdhouse according to diagram.	
7. Wash out the paintbrushes.	
8. Put paintbrushes away.	
9. Clean up work area.	

Fig. 6.17

CONTRACT

TASK

Who: Jenna

What: Feed and walk the dog

When: every day

How Well: Jenna will feed and walk the dog every day after dinner. Must do this for 10 days to earn reward

REWARD

Who: Mom

What: Out for dinner

When: after 10 days (10 days in a row)

How Much: Jenna can pick any restaurant and have dinner with mom

Sign here: _____   Date: _____

Sign here: _____   Date: _____

TASK RECORD

M	T	W	Th	F	Sa	Su	M	T	W	Th	F	Sa	Su

it onto the calendar, working backwards from the due date. This approach makes it very clear to the student what needs to be done and when it needs to be done. Each day she can only work on the aspect of the project that is noted on the calendar. This helps her focus her attention to the task at hand and not become distracted by other elements of the project. Calendars can be used to plan out big projects (such as term papers or science projects) or for multi-step activities such as packing for a trip.

Using Visual Supports to Increase Motivation

Mrs. Rodriguez took her ten-year old son with autism, Carlos, for an educational evaluation. The evaluator suggested using graphic organizers/word maps to first help Carlos organize his thoughts and then use as a reference for social interactions. After a trip to the zoo, Mrs. Rodriguez sat down with her son and proceeded to develop a graphic organizer, depicting the day's events. It was titled "Our Trip to the Zoo" and contained information about the animals they saw, what the animals were doing, and information they gained about the animals, as well as other activities of the day. Mrs. Rodriguez sent Carlos to school the next day with the graphic organizer and asked that the speech therapist use it to discuss the trip. Once he understood how to use the organizer, Carlos began to read what was on it and was tickled by the fact that he could relate what he had experienced.

Over time, Carlos's mother and the educational staff developed other ways to use graphic organizers with him. Using this visual support gave Carlos a means of interacting with others and resulted in better eye contact, less stereotypic verbal behavior, and increased interest in others. It opened the door for mutually enjoyable social interactions—something he hadn't experienced before.

Have you ever been asked to learn to do something difficult, something you know will be a struggle to accomplish? Do you remember how that felt? I am sure you can quickly come up with several experiences without much thought. Why? It is because you tend to remember experiences that were really difficult or really wonderful with great ease. Think about our students with autism. Every day is a struggle to accomplish something new. It is no wonder that motivation or lack of motivation plays an important role in skill acquisition.

This chapter addresses the role that reinforcement can play in motivating students with autism. More specifically, positive reinforcement will be the focus of this chapter. Positive reinforcement (providing reinforcement contingent upon performing a specific behavior) is effective in increasing target behaviors. Developing systems to motivate our learners and to establish ourselves as the givers of reinforcement is critical to successful learning.

There are many ways to provide reinforcement. Reinforcement systems may start out as an artificial means of letting the individual know that something good will happen in return for his efforts. As the student ages, particularly in adolescence and adulthood, it is important to consider natural contingencies (i.e., rewards) provided by the community. If you adjust your reinforcement to mirror reinforcement provided outside of the educational setting, you increase your options for reinforcement exponentially. For example, reinforcement can come in the form of a smile from the librarian when returning a book or a greeting from a cashier in a local grocery store.

Natural contingencies are most likely to be rewarding if social reinforcement becomes a conditioned reinforcer (that is, one that is not initially reinforcing, but comes so through experience). The community readily provides conditioned reinforcers. On the other hand, I don't know of any community where the members carry baggies of food reinforcement to be doled out on a planned schedule or tokens to be placed on a token board. These types of reinforcement systems are a great start, but they most certainly cannot be the end result.

This chapter will cover the following issues related to increasing a child's motivation:

- Letting the child know **who** will be providing the reinforcement (when the student prefers particular people in his environment or when reinforcement will be provided by someone other than the person who is teaching him)
- Determining **what** the child is motivated by or selecting reinforcement preferences (which is important for any student)
- Deciding **where** reinforcement will be received (when specific locations are preferred or the reinforcement will occur in another location)
- Letting the learner know **when** reinforcement is coming (which is especially important when you are beginning to increase the time between initiation of instruction and the reinforcement)
- Deciding **how much** reinforcement will be received (important if the task requires significant effort)
- Helping the child understand **why** he should engage in the task (explaining the long-term benefits)

You need not incorporate all of these aspects into your reinforcement system. The simpler the system, the easier it is for the student to understand. There may be specific aspects of reinforcement that are of particular interest to your student. Assess what is important to him and choose the strategies that fit best. This may take some ongoing modification, but is well worth the effort. A motivated student is a happy and successful student!

Important Principles of Providing Reinforcement

There are a few general considerations to follow when providing reinforcement:

- When the student is learning something new, reinforcement should be continuous (i.e., one reinforcer for each response).
- As the student begins to understand the task, reinforcement can be thinned out slowly (i.e., every two responses, then every three responses, etc.).
- Next, reinforcement should be provided sporadically—on a random, unpredictable schedule such as a variable interval (varying the amount of time between rewards) or a variable ratio schedule (varying the number of tasks or commands that must be followed in order to earn reinforcement).
- You need to know what the individual wants at any given learning opportunity. (This is known as the *reinforcement appetite* or *motivating operation*.)
    - This can change from moment to moment. For example, at first, pieces of candy or another food may be very motivating for the child, but as his appetite for the food is satisfied, he will become less motivated to work for it.
    - It may require some time to investigate other possible reinforcers when current options don't seem enticing any more.
    - It will depend on how long it has been since the specific reinforcer has been presented in the past and how much of the reinforcement the student has already received. (Reinforcement is less powerful after frequent exposure.)
- The amount, quality, and intensity of reinforcement should match the amount of effort it takes the person to do the task (e.g., shoveling an entire driveway should yield greater reinforcement than shoveling a small section of the sidewalk).
- Move from artificial reinforcement systems to natural reinforcement contingencies (a trip to the ice cream shop, a trip to the video store, high fives, smiles, praise statements, an allowance, or a break or free time, to name a few) when the person is ready.

VISUALIZE THIS: IDEAS, IDEAS, IDEAS

What????

Before you can provide reinforcement to a student, you need to know what is reinforcing to him. We recommend doing formal or informal preference assessments in order to build a menu that is large enough to keep reinforcement novel. The reader can refer to *Incentives for Change* (Delmolino & Harris, 2004) for detailed information on how to determine what is reinforcing for a particular individual with ASD.

Tangible items are probably the most common form of reinforcement for learners with autism. Having a visual representation of the object can help with motivation as it shows the student *"what"* he is trying to earn.

Fig. 7.1

Objects or Pictures

It can be helpful to put the reinforcement where the student can see it to help remind him what he is working toward (see Figure 7.1). For some students, the actual item on the table may be too distracting. In that case, you can substitute a picture of the item or a written reminder of what the reward is, as shown in Figure 7.2.

Token Systems

If a student is able to understand the concept of earning points, tokens, or other intrinsically worthless items that can be exchanged for things or activities he wants, a token system can be an important motivational tool. Use a token system to keep a learner on track and focused on "what" the reinforcement will be.

Token systems can come in a variety of forms. Every token system should be created for the individual, keeping in mind personal preferences. The first step is to determine what form the tokens will be in: for example, coins, stickers, or poker chips. Then decide how many tokens will be required to "purchase" a back-up reinforcer (what the student will receive in exchange for the token). When first teaching a child to use a token system, start small. It is usually best to require him to earn only one token that he can exchange immediately for a desired item.

The example of a token system pictured in Figure 7.3 shows what back-up reinforcer the student will earn when he accumulates all of the necessary tokens. See *Incentives for Change* (Delmolino and Harris, 2004) for more information about implementing an effective token economy.

Fig. 7.2

cookies

**Finish work
and earn
cookies.**

Fig. 7.3

Puzzle Boards

One variation of a traditional token board that can be a useful visual support for students with ASD is the puzzle board. To use this system, cut a picture of the desired reinforcer (e.g., a magazine) into pieces. Each piece of the "puzzle" then serves as a token. Then, determine the criteria for earning a piece of the puzzle (i.e., completing a task). Upon completion of the task, the learner will earn a token (puzzle piece). In the example in Figure 7.4, when the puzzle is completed, the tokens (puzzle pieces) are exchanged for the object or event depicted.

Using this strategy provides the student with a visual image of the backup reinforcer that he is working toward earning. As he earns more pieces, he can see how close he is to receiving the reinforcement.

Fig. 7.4

How Much??

It may be unclear to some students how they can earn reinforcers. Use these visual strategies to show them that by completing a specific type or amount of work, they can earn different amounts of reinforcement. These examples can be modified to meet the individual abilities of any child or adult.

Task Chart

A task chart lists different jobs that can be completed for rewards. This system allows the individual more flexibility in determining how much work he needs to do in order to purchase different reinforcers. In the example shown in Figure 7.5, the student earns one key for successfully completing a task. The chart shows how much work (keys earned) the student must complete to earn reach reward. The student can decide if he wants to "cash-in" or keep earning keys for a larger reinforcer.

Systems Using Money as Reinforcement

You can use a combination of strategies, charts, and banking to help the individual determine how much effort he must exert to earn the money he needs to purchase an item of his choice. The chart pictured in Figure 7.6 on the next page provides an example of different types of chores that can be completed. The chart shows pictures of each chore, how often it can be completed (daily, weekly, or monthly), and how much can be earned for the job. Each picture is attached with Velcro™ so it can be removed from the chart once the chore is completed and replaced with different chores.

Fig. 7.5

Job List

- Stuff and label 25 envelopes
- File for 15 minutes
- Wash and dry towels
- Vacuum 4 offices
- Clean 6 tables and counter tops
- Empty dishwasher and put dishes away
- Collect trash from all rooms and take to dumpster

- Shred paper for 15 minutes
- Assemble 20 travel kits
- Wash windows in café
- Load Dishwasher
- Wash 24 chairs
- Sweep floor in café

Soda	Read a magazine (5 min)	Listen to music (10 min)	Use computer (15 min)
Candy	Draw with markers (5 min)	Go for a walk	Play video game (15 min)
Puzzle	Walk on treadmill (5 min)	Play game with friend	Watch TV (15 min)
			Talk with staff member (15 min)

Fig. 7.6

Fig. 7.7

Figure 7.7 at left is a visual reminder for the student of his ultimate goal. The banking system (Figure 7.8 on page 107) enables the student to see his savings grow as he works on achieving his goal. It is set up like a traditional checking or savings passbook.

■ Who??

Everyone has preferences in regard to other people. There are certain people we like talking to or working with, or whose company we simply enjoy. Some children and adults with ASD are motivated by knowing that they can get access to certain people. They may be motivated to work on a complicated activity if they know they will be able to spend time with a specific person.

The strategy below will be helpful for students who need to see "who" will be providing their reinforcement.

Photographs

Photographs can help the student determine *"who"* he wants to receive reinforcement from. They can also be used to indicate that reinforcement will be provided by someone other than the instructor.

Create reinforcement boards with photographs of the different people in the environment who can provide reinforcement. Be sure to select only those individuals who are available to provide reinforcement at the correct time. In other words, do not select someone who might be out of the building, absent, or engaged in an activity that cannot be interrupted. The students can then choose the person with

Fig. 7.8

Date	Description	Deposit	Withdrawal	Balance	
4/20/04	Walk dog	1.00			
					1.00
4/20/04	Feed cat	.50		+	.50
					1.50
4/21/04	Mow lawn	10.00		+	10.00
					11.50
4/22/04	Sweep kitchen	1.00		+	1.00
					12.50
4/22/04	Wash dishes	1.00		+	1.00
					13.50
4/22/04	Feed cat	.50		+	.50
					14.00
4/22/04	Walk dog	1.00		+	1.00
					15.00
				+	

whom they would most like to engage in an activity, event, or conversation. See Figure 7.9 for an example.

Fig. 7.9

When??

Some children and adults with ASD get frustrated if they are not sure when they will receive their reinforcement. Concrete representations that show "when" they will earn the chosen item or activity will greatly reduce anxiety. For example, you can make it crystal clear to the individual that "first you set the table, then you can play outside."

Activity Schedules

Some students may need a visual cue to understand when reinforcement will be available. For younger students, activity schedules are often made with small, three-ring binders. A picture of one activity is glued or Velcroed to each page, and the student flips over each page as he completes the activity (Figure 7.10). Pictures of rewards are interspersed among the pictures of activities, and the student learns that he may have the reward when he completes the activities on the preceding pages.

Fig. 7.10

For older students, a simple picture schedule can be created by mounting a strip of Velcro™ (hook side) onto a clipboard, manila folder, or sturdy paper for the base of the schedule. Then, take photographs of tasks, activities, and other potential reinforcing items. Laminate the pictures and attach a piece of Velcro (loop side) to the back of each. The activity tasks should be arranged in order (top to bottom or left to right), leaving space at the end of the schedule for the student

Fig. 7.11

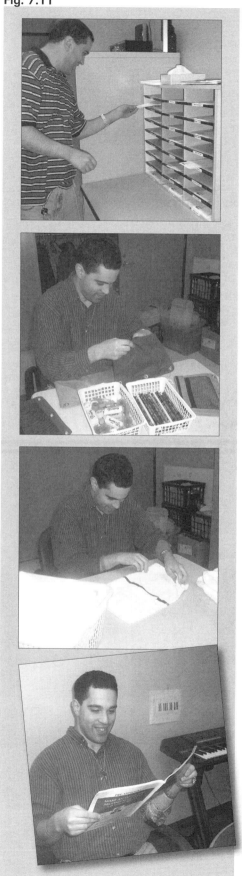

to place the photograph of the desired reinforcement (Figure 7.11). The student can then see the tasks or activities he must complete before he earns his chosen reward.

Color Cues

Color cues can be used on written schedules to highlight when reinforcement is available. In the example in Figure 7.12 in the color insert, the individual's routine activities are typed in black and the scheduled reinforcing activities are typed in red. The red typeface directs the learner's attention to that particular timeframe to highlight when the reinforcement will occur.

Blank templates can be provided for students who are able to create their own schedules. This template can have specific blocks or cells that are colored (e.g., yellow) to prompt the student to schedule a reinforcing activity or event for himself during that period of time.

Clocks and Timers

A digital kitchen timer or a clock can be used to draw attention to when reinforcement will be available. For example, the teacher might tell a student, "After you read for 20 minutes we will go outside," then set a timer so the student will see when the end of the interval is approaching.

Visual timers are helpful for those who do not understand traditional timers or clocks. One type of visual timer has a colored wheel (instead of numbers) that decreases in size as time passes. See Figures 5.1a-5.1c in the color insert for examples of visual timers, and the Resources at the end of the book for information on where this type of timer can be purchased.

Token Systems

Token systems can be used to highlight "when" reinforcement will come. In the example shown below (Figure 7.13), when all of the tokens (pennies) are on the board, the student will receive reinforcement. Again, when the student is first learning to use a token system, begin by requiring him to earn only a small number of tokens to receive a reward and then gradually increase the number needed. Initially, give a token for short periods of appropriate behavior or task completion. Use tokens the student likes, but that are not primarily reinforcing alone, or he will not be especially interested in earning other reinforcers in exchange for the tokens. See the references at the end of the chapter for more information about implementing an effective token economy.

Fig. 7.13

Another example of a token system is shown in Figure 7.14. In this example, a thermometer is used to indicate when the reinforcement will be earned. Use Velcro™ to attach the pieces to the thermometer. The number of pieces used can be individualized based upon the child's ability and the size/magnitude of the reinforcer he is working toward. The criteria for how each individual piece of the thermometer (token) will be earned should be predetermined. This should be clear to the child so he understands how he will acquire each piece. For example, he might receive a piece of the thermometer upon successfully completing his homework assignments each night. When each piece is in place and fills the thermometer, he receives the reinforcement indicated. In the example shown in Figure 7.14, after the child earns 8 pieces and fills the thermometer, he will earn a trip to Great Adventure.

Where?

Some children and adults with ASD are particular about **"where"** they will be able to do the activities they have earned. Although the teacher may tell a child where he will have his snack break, it may not be evident

Fig. 7.14

to the child without a visual cue. The examples below show how to highlight the location of reinforcement

Written Schedules

Helping someone remember where reinforcement will occur is important when the person prefers specific locations or when the reinforcement will occur in an alternate location. For example, the student may earn the opportunity to work on the computer but the location may vary from the classroom—perhaps sometimes in the office or sometimes in the computer lab. If the student uses a written schedule, you (or the student) can write the location of his reinforcement into his schedule, perhaps using color to highlight this information. A picture schedule can provide the same information to students who cannot read.

Photographs

Take photographs of different locations where the individual may receive his reinforcement (classroom, gym, or playground). Laminate the photographs and attach Velcro™ so the pictures can be easily changed. The example in Figure 7.15 shows the learner "WHERE" reinforcement will occur.

Fig. 7.15

▨ Why??

"Why do I have to do homework?" "Why do I have to make my bed?" "Why can't I eat candy?" If you know an inquisitive learner like this, who wants answers to his questions, then these strategies can help you. These suggestions may take some time to develop, but the long-tem effects will alleviate the stress of having to respond to "why, why, why?"

Power Cards

As discussed in Chapter 2, Power Cards capitalize on a student's special interest to motivate and attract his attention. Any real person or imaginary character the student likes can be featured on a Power Card and explain WHY the learner should do certain things. For example, if the child enjoys watching Pokemon cartoons, use that interest to make a card explaining why he has to take a shower every night. This information can be presented on a small index card.

The student can keep the file card in his wallet for reference. The pros and cons of why you are required to do certain things can be pointed out if appropriate. For example, to clarify why your child must complete household chores, the Power Card can explain that he will earn an allowance for doing his chores at home. Earning an allowance gives him the opportunity to purchase the things he likes.

Social Stories

Social Stories are used to explain concepts or areas of misconception to the children and adults with ASD. These stories are written in language the individual can comprehend. For example, to help a student understand WHY he should do his school work, a Social Story can explain the benefits of doing your homework or listening to the teacher, highlighting the positives of doing these things.

Social Stories should be reviewed and discussed with the student daily. Some learners can be actively involved in developing the story.

Using Visual Supports to Increase Social Skills

Samantha was a teen who found physical touch unpleasant. When a new person approached her and put out his or her hand to shake, she would pull away. Most people interpreted this behavior as a sign that Samantha did not want to interact. This was not the message that she wanted to give to other people, however. We used a visual cue of a photo to help her learn an alternative way of handling handshakes. The photo depicted Samantha greeting her teacher with a conversation bubble over the teacher's head that said "Nice to meet you" and a conversation bubble over her own head saying "I have a cold and so I don't want to shake your hand." By reviewing this photo daily, Samantha was eventually able to greet new people in a way that was not perceived as offensive. This was a simple solution to a problem that was hindering interactions with new people.

One of the most critical areas of functioning for children and adults with ASD is social skills. Unfortunately, all of the instruction done in other areas of learning will not ensure that new skills are directly transferred to the social arena. Social skill development is so complex and the social skills used with one person in one setting may be entirely different from those that need to be used with another person in another setting. Consequently, we believe that these skills cannot be effectively taught in the learning environment alone.

So, what are we aiming for? It is not reasonable to think that our students will pick up on the specifics of every interaction. It is reasonable, however, to expect that they can learn to adjust to the wonderful variety of skills that exist in the real world. Placing a young or inexperienced student immediately into real world situations before she has had systematic instruction may not be the place to start. However, this type of education is essential for older students.

In our experience, exposing individuals with autism to humor and give-and-take dialog helps them to adjust to, and participate in, a wider variety of interactions. It is such an enormous pleasure to see people with ASD react to jokes with a smile or a laugh and even more so for them to begin to joke with us. Once a person with autism is able to understand the learning environment, more natural interactions should be slowly introduced into the informal instructional time of the day.

There are a myriad of social skills to be considered. Covering all of them piece by piece would be impossible. The flow chart below touches on some of the major areas in order of complexity.

This chapter will cover some ideas for the use of visual supports for each area.

Fig. 8.1

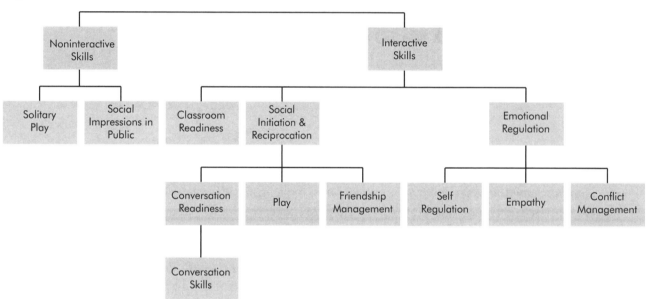

VISUALIZE THIS: IDEAS, IDEAS, IDEAS

 ## Non-Interactive Social Skills

Solitary Play

Most typically developing children above the age of five or six can entertain themselves for hours without direct supervision or instruction from an adult. In contrast, although some students with autism may enjoy being by themselves, the activities they choose to do are not always appropriate or productive. These learners need cues to help guide their choices, which will teach them how to spend their free time more appropriately.

Activity Schedules

Drs. Lynn McClannahan and Patricia Krantz (1999) describe activity schedules as "a set of pictures or words that cues someone to engage in a sequence of activities." An important use of activity schedules is to enable individuals with autism to play independently.

When a child is first learning to use an activity schedule, she might be asked to do just one solitary activity before receiving reinforcement. For example, an early activity schedule might consist of a photo of a puzzle mounted on one page

Fig. 8.2

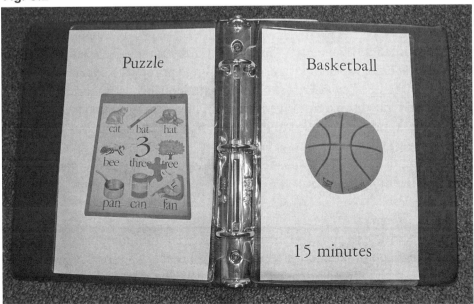

in a binder, followed by a photo of a reinforcer such as a snack. First with prompting, and then independently, the student would turn to the photo of the puzzle, get the puzzle from its storage area and put it together, and then approach an adult for her snack. Once she can follow the photo cues independently, additional activities would be added to her schedule.

Teaching a student with autism how to use an activity schedule allows her to engage in a solitary play or leisure activity independently. Eventually, some students not only learn to do leisure activities independently, but also to organize their own free time. For more information on the creation and implementation of activity schedules see *Activity Schedules for Children with Autism.*

Video Models

Video models can be used to teach solitary play skills such as doll play, playing with cars or trucks, or putting a puzzle together. Video models are especially helpful if the child has an interest in a particular toy, but does not use it the way intended or for extended periods of time.

Make a videotape of a child playing with the toy appropriately. The videotape should be short in length (1 to 2 minutes) and the "actor" should model typical behavior that you want the child with ASD to learn. Have the child watch the video several times per day. It is a good idea to show the video before the child is scheduled for a play session/experience.

Social Impressions in Public

It is important to help every child or adult with ASD acquire skills that will improve the social impressions that they make in their communities. After all, the ultimate goal is for them to be integrated into the community for education, recreational activities, and employment. In the community, people judge each other based upon the way they look or how they act. For individuals with autism, however, knowing what to say, how to dress, or how to interact with others does not always come naturally. The suggestions below may make these skills more attainable.

Power Cards

As explained in Chapter 2, "The Power Card strategy is a visual aid that incorporates the child's special interest in teaching appropriate social interactions" (Gagnon, 2001). Use Power Cards to remind students of the importance of social behaviors that may have a negative impact on how others perceive them. For example, Power Cards can be used to remind someone to use a napkin, use a tissue, or to chew with her mouth closed. For detailed information about designing and implementing this strategy, please refer to *Power Cards* by Elisa Gagnon (see Recommended Reading, page 156).

Photo Boards

Photo boards use photographs of clothes from an individual's wardrobe to help her select coordinated outfits more independently. Figure 8.3 (color insert) shows an example of a color-coded photo board. The pictures of the shirts and pants that match are glued onto the same color of paper. There may be some shirts

Fig. 8.4

Mark's Bathroom Rules

Sometimes I really have to go to the bathroom!!

When I am finished going, I sometimes forget something VERY important...

To zip up!!

When I am finished in the bathroom I must :

STOP!

THINK!

AND REMEMBER......ZIP UP!

No one likes it when I walk around with my pants unzipped.

When I remember to zip up my friends will be so happy!!!

Yeah for me, I remembered to keep my pants zipped!!

that can be worn with different pants (e.g., t-shirts with jeans or sweats), so duplicate pictures will need to be made. The child can select the type of pants he or she wants to wear and match it with a shirt that has the same color code.

This photo board uses removable cards that are backed with Velcro. After each clothing item is worn, its photo is taken from the board and is not returned until the item has been laundered.

Social Stories™

As discussed throughout the book, Social Stories™ are used to clarify topics the learner with ASD may misunderstand. These stories are written in language the student can comprehend. Some students can be actively involved in the development of the story.

Social Stories should be reviewed with the learner daily to provide opportunities to review and discuss important details or topics. Social Stories can be written to clarify appropriate social behavior in public (e.g., burping, speaking with your mouth full, or personal hygiene). The example shown in Figure 8.4 on the previous page uses simple language and icons or photographs to illustrate the importance of zipping your pants.

■ Interactive Social Skills

Classroom Readiness

To be successful in the classroom, students must be able to demonstrate basic readiness skills. Some common expectations for students include the ability to sit quietly, attend to the teacher, and follow simple directions. The following examples can be used to assist children who have difficulty demonstrating classroom readiness skills independently.

Fig. 8.5

Class Rules

1. Raise your hand.

2. Look at the teacher.

3. Use inside voice to talk.

Fig. 8.6

Power Cards

A Power Card can be created to cue the student into the importance of sitting quietly in class and looking at the teacher. The Power Card can be placed on the student's desk for easy reference. Eventually, a small picture of the hero can be used alone to remind the student to stay focused. For example, if a student likes Princess Leia from the *Star Wars* series, she might be initially given a Power Card with a picture of Princess Leia as well as a reminder from Princess Leia to sit quietly and keep her eyes on the teacher. Later, a picture of Princess Leia alone may be enough to cue her to sit quietly and watch the teacher. (See references for more information.)

Cue Cards and Charts

Cue cards and charts can be created to help students understand the classroom rules. Charts are combinations of written words and icons to briefly explain the rules. The charts can be posted in the classroom for all students, or a smaller version can be created for individual desks. Figure 8.5 shows an example of Class Rules. Figure 8.6 shows how a cue card (STOP) placed on the bathroom door can indicate that the bathroom is occupied. Cue cards can be single words on a card or symbols and pictures.

Be aware that after awhile, the student might get used to particular cue cards or chards posted on her desk or on the board and stop paying attention to them. If so, change the card visually in some way to ensure it continues to attract the student's attention.

◾ Social Initiation and Reciprocation

Conversation Readiness Skills

Some students with ASD enjoy talking to peers, parents, or teachers but may not have the skills necessary to engage in meaningful conversations. They may forget (or may not know) some key skills related to conversations, such as: how to start a conversation, how to sustain it, and how to end it. The visual strategies in this section can be used as aids for an individual with limited skills or for one who becomes anxious when engaged in conversation with others.

Written Scripts

Written scripts can be used to help students participate in conversations using different phrases. The idea is for the student to read from the scripts in the beginning and later on commit the phrases/questions to memory. The cards can be color coded: green for greetings, yellow for conversation starters, and red for conversation enders. Create different cards with several different phrases and occasionally mix them up so the student will use different greetings and closing statements.

Introduce written scripts first in structured classroom conversations, such as between two students sitting together at the lunch table. Later, encourage the student to use her written scripts in less structured settings, such as before or after class or with someone who hasn't been trained to respond to written scripts. Initially, present the individual with a set of cards that guide her through a conversation. For example, one written script for a greeting may say, "Hey! What's up?"; the conversation starter script might say, "What did you do last night?"; and the conversation ender might say "Nice talking to you. I've got to get back to work." A variety of scripts should be prepared for each category so that conversation is more natural. As the student becomes competent with the cards, gradually reduce their size and begin to fade their use completely.

Graphic Organizers

For students with autism who can read, graphic organizers can help them understand different ways to start a conversation. The example shown in Figure 8.7 identifies main topics that the student can use as a reference in generating questions that can sustain a meaningful conversation. The student may initially have to carry the card around as an immediate visual cue (while practicing at first with familiar people). Later, the card can serve as a review prior to an op-

Fig. 8.7

Starting Conversations

Ask about the PRESENT
"What are you doing/reading/eating?"

Ask about the PAST
"How was your weekend/lunch/vacation?"

Ask about the FUTURE
"What are you going to do tomorrow/later?"

Ask about their INTERESTS
"Have you been to the movies/playing a sport/ working on a craft project?"

Adapted from Jed Baker, Social Skills Training Project

portunity to converse. Finally, the card can be eliminated or new cards can be introduced. Some learners may be able to brainstorm and think of their own ideas for beginning a conversation.

Cue Cards

Talk show hosts, actors, and telemarketers all rely on the use of cue cards to ensure that the conversation and interaction between them and their "audience" will flow in a natural manner. Children and adults with autism spectrum disorders can benefit from the use of cue cards in settings where they are required to ask questions. For example, when younger children participate in *Show & Tell* activities, they can use cue cards with questions they can ask their peers (such as "Where did you get it?," "What does it do?," "Who gave it to you?"). Older students could use such cards when asking classmates questions about their science presentations or when learning how to make small talk in the cafeteria. The teacher or a paraprofessional can hold the cards, or the student can do so. This will allow her to actively participate in the activity.

Charts

Icons can be used on charts that highlight key points and important facts the learner needs to remember. For example, you can create a chart that reminds students how to share a lab desk in science (keep some distance between you and your lab partner, ask for materials you need to share, clean up your lab project). You can also do something similar to teach the student to work on group social studies projects together by listing those rules.

Photo Cards

A student with ASD who likes to talk about one particular topic (e.g., maps, telephone poles, car models and makes) regardless of whether listeners are interested can benefit from the introduction of photo cards. The photos could show the facial expressions of listeners when they are interested in the conversation (eye contact, smiling, nodding); are becoming tired of the subject (head in hand, yawning, loss of eye contact); or have lost interest all together (rolling their eyes, making faces, doing something else).

The photo cards can first be introduced in role play with the teacher and other adults. You can have the student hold the photo cards and try to match them with her communication partner's expressions. Or, the partner can hold the cards and show them to the student to indicate her emotions related to the conversation (for example, by showing the "bored" photo card when she is getting bored). Later, the teacher can review an interaction that just occurred by pointing out the person's response during conversation and relating that to the photos. Eventually, the student can be taught to self-monitor her performance.

Play

Play is an important part of everyone's life. Knowing how to play with your peers appropriately is critical for ensuring positive social interactions. Sharing, taking turns, waiting, and asking to join in are a few of the many play skills all children need to understand and readily demonstrate in order to make and keep friends. Using the strategies suggested below can help students with ASD imitate the desired play skills that are demonstrated by age-appropriate models.

Social Stories

A digital camera and some "actors" are all you will need to create your own pictorial Social Story. These Social Stories can be used to teach children the right and wrong way to deal with difficult play situations. For instance, you can write and illustrate stories about the need to share toys, wait your turn for the slide, or play fairly.

Your story should briefly cover good and bad ways to handle the given play situation. It should also show the outcome of both right and wrong patterns of behavior. *The Social Skills Picture Book* by Jed Baker (2003) has many examples that depict play-related skills. You can create stories based upon a child's individual needs and visually highlight the pictures of children in the *Social Skills Picture Book* who are doing desirable things.

Video Models

A video model can be created to show children how to appropriately use such social skills as cleaning up toys, sharing toys, taking turns, using inside and outside voices, listening when someone is talking, and observing personal space. The videotape should be relatively short in length (one to two minutes) and should clearly illustrate the desired behavior. The models can be same-aged peers or adult models (parent and teachers) who role play the desired behavior or action. Before producing the video, create a script for the models (actors) so they know what to say and do and then start recording your video.

The benefit of a good video is that a consistent lesson is portrayed each time it is viewed. In addition, multiple students can benefit from watching the same video.

Fig. 8.8

Cue Cards

Cue cards can be used instead of videos to demonstrate appropriate play skills. For nonreaders, a cue card might consist of a photograph or symbol on a card meant to cue appropriate behavior. For example, to remind a child to wait at the bottom of the slide for her turn, a cue card showing a photo of the child standing at the bottom of the slide might be made. The recess aide or parent volunteer could hold it up when the children are waiting in line.

For a reader, cue cards consist of a couple of words of reminder written on a card. Figure 8.8 illustrates a card used to signal a child who can read when it is time to take a turn when playing a game.

Friendship Management

If asked to name some characteristics of a good friend, we might say someone who is nice, knows how to share, can take turns, and is honest and dependable. Many students with autism, however, would be hard pressed to identify these characteristics. Making friends and sustaining that friendship is challenging for individuals with autism. The different aspects of friendship are concepts that do not always receive direct instruction. Understanding the "rules" of friendship can be clarified by using the suggestion explained below.

Photographs and Videos

Photographs and videos are excellent tools to illustrate important social skills every child or adult needs to maintain friendships. Video modeling can be used to teach students with ASD more about sharing, taking turns or teasing, or photographs can be used to show the right and wrong way to acquire and sustain friendships (Baker, 2003). You can also use photographs and videos to develop supports for friendship skills such as smiling at people, making eye contact, laughing at their jokes, and telling your own jokes.

Graphic Organizers

You can create a graphic organizer specifically listing traits of a good friend (keeps secrets, is helpful in solving problems, takes turns, respects your property, etc.). You could also create a graphic organizer listing the traits of someone who is *not* a friend (laughs when you get hurt, calls you names, breaks your toys, etc.). After you observe an interaction in which the child uses appropriate or inappropriate social skills, it is helpful to review the graphic organizer with her and see if she can identify what she did right (or wrong).

Fig. 8.9

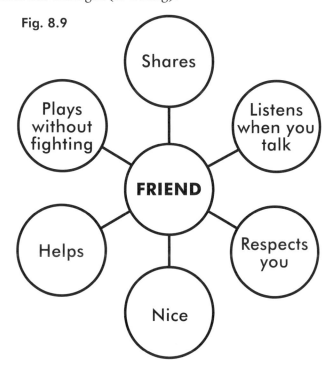

■ Emotional Regulation

Self-Regulation

Experiencing events such as death, moving to a new home, or going to the doctor can cause a variety of negative emotions (e.g., anxiety, stress, or sadness). Some students with ASD may not be able to tell us that they are experiencing stress or sadness, but as parents and teachers we know possible events that could trigger these feelings.

The goal is to help the student *regulate* her emotions (avoiding extreme reactions when they are not warranted). For example, if a student is sensitive to cigarette smoke, an inappropriate response would be to dramatize her reaction by throwing herself to the floor and making a choking sound. More appropriate ways of expressing her feelings might include leaving the area quietly or politely asking the smoker to stop. The individual can still express her emotion, but without being disruptive or offensive. Planning ahead and being proactive is the key for making the intervention effective.

Fig. 8.10

My Friend Allan

Allan's wife had two babies. Their names are Kaitlyn and Jeremy.

He has to help care for the babies. It is a lot of work.

Allan is home with the babies.

When the babies are a little older, Allan will come back to work with me on February 19.

I can look at my calendar and see when Allan will come back.

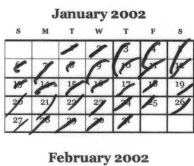

Social Stories

Social Stories (Gray, 1995) can be used to help students learn to cope appropriately with a variety of emotions. For example, they can help students who experience anxiety when they do not understand why different events occur. A Social Story can help them by giving suggestions for dealing with anxiety or stress in an appropriate manner. For example, Figure 8.10 is a Social Story that clarifies why someone important in a student's life has gone and explains what he is doing. A calendar at the end of the story allows the student to cross off the days until the person returns.

Social Stories could also be written to help students learn to deal appropriately with anger, fear, frustration, boredom, etc. The key is for you to recognize that the child needs help learning to handle a particular emotion in a particular situation and then to develop a story showing her a better way to react in that situation. As always, the story should be written in language that the child can understand. It should be reviewed with her daily, giving her the opportunity to discuss her concerns.

I don't need to be sad because Allan will be back. He will be my teacher again.

If I want to talk to Allan I can call him on the phone.

Social Story Questions—Adam S.

After the story has been read with Adam, ask him a few questions regarding the story. The ideas below can be modified in any way. Be careful not to ask the same questions each time the story is read or ask them in the same order.

Is Allan coming back to work with you?

Where is Allan?

Why is he at home?

When is Allan coming back?

If you miss Allan what can you do?

Should you be sad because Allan is not here?

Emotion Charts

Emotion charts can help children identify emotions they are feeling (happy, sad, confused). Initially, a parent or teacher would need to prompt the child to identify a particular emotion by pairing the emotion with the picture. One example would be to prompt the child to point to a picture of a sad face and say "You're crying; you must be sad." If the child has trouble relating stylized drawings of faces to facial expressions on real people, take pictures of the child herself (or someone else in her life) when she is expressing different emotions.

Fig. 8.11

▓ Empathy

Many children with autism spectrum disorders do not demonstrate "theory of mind." That is, they do not understand that other people may have opinions, thoughts, or feelings that differ from their own. These children often seem indifferent to other people's distress—that is, they do not show empathy. Other children with ASD do recognize others' distress, but do not know how to respond to it appropriately (Bacon, Fein, Morris, et al., 1998). It is easy to understand why students with autism are challenged by another person's emotions, but there are visual supports that can help them learn to empathize with others.

Photos

Having empathy for somebody else can be a challenge if the learner cannot "read" the facial expressions or body language of others. It may help to take photographs of people making different expressions in context. For example, take a photo of a sad child with a broken toy, or an angry woman looking at mud tracked all over her kitchen floor. The concrete examples help to create a connection between feelings and events. As a future step, you can take photographs of people making different faces or posing with different body postures that might represent several emotions. The learner can pair the photograph with a description of what that particular face/body posture might indicate.

Graphic Organizers

If you have identified areas where your child has difficulty expressing empathy, you can make a graphic organizer to help her know how to respond in given situations. For example, perhaps she does not know how to respond if a smaller child is crying, or if her mother is angry, or if a friend is scared. Knowing how to show emotion appropriately can be challenging.

Some children with ASD may benefit from a graphic organizer illustrating the situations in which it is appropriate to show you care when someone else is hurt, crying, or expressing another negative emotion, as well as situations in which it is appropriate to respond to someone who is expressing happiness, pride, or another positive emotion. A graphic organizer can list a number of examples for each emotion. Examples that directly relate to the child's own life would be helpful in establishing a connection.

The example in Figure 8.12 illustrates how to show people you care and could be used to cue a child with ASD to show empathy appropriately. Additional stems off the main idea can be left blank for the child to fill in with her own ideas.

Fig. 8.12

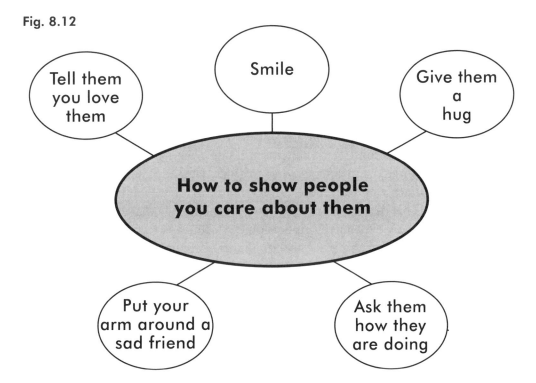

Video Models

Another way to demonstrate emotions is to create video models depicting events that can be related to specific emotions. The actors can talk about a particular event that is being taped and state how the event makes them feel. For example, you can videotape a situation where property was destroyed and the owner verbalizes that he is angry. A variety of examples for each emotion should be videotaped so the child can learn from multiple examples. This will help with generalization.

Conflict Management

At one time or another, we all must deal with conflict. If handled inappropriately, these interactions can cause stress or perhaps even more conflict. Teaching conflict management to people with ASD is challenging. There are, however, several visual strategies that can effectively show someone with ASD how to handle these situations in a positive manner that will end the verbal or physical conflict.

Comic Strip Conversations

Comic Strip Conversations (Gray, 1994) incorporate the use of simple drawings and color to illustrate the dialogue between two or more people. They are helpful for individuals who have difficulty comprehending the quick exchange of conversation. Comic Strip Conversations can be created by the teacher or the teacher and the student. The dialogue is written in different colors to indicate the suggested meanings or emotions associated with the words (for example: happy statements are green, confusion is represented by a mixture of colors, red symbolizes anger, purple is proud, blue symbolizes sad, and black is factual information).

Figure 8.13 (color insert) illustrates a conversation between two children. The student with ASD can use the Comic Strip Conversation to help her understand a confusing interaction with another child.

Video Modeling

As previously discussed, video modeling and photographs can be beneficial aids to clarify social interactions for children and adults with autism. They can be used to teach about conflict management if you create videos with same-aged peers or teachers engaged in some type of conflict. The video should be short and show an appropriate way to handle an argument or other conflict. For example, George spills his drink on Brenda's new portable DVD player. On the video, Brenda may state how expensive this equipment is and ask that George not eat or drink near her DVD player again. Another example might include having George apologize and offer to pay for repairs that might be needed.

These videos can be reviewed often and can facilitate discussions about how to deal with similar situations. Photographs can also be incorporated into stories or photo-boards that show the right and wrong way to deal with arguments, fights, or other conflicts (Baker, 2003).

Power Cards

Power Cards can also be used to teach a student how to handle conflict appropriately. A favorite cartoon character (for example, Sponge Bob or Dora the Explorer) could be illustrated on a card. Examples showing the child's hero doing things such as counting to ten, taking some deep breaths, or other relaxation techniques can provide an incentive for the child to use these appropriate responses during times of conflict.

Strategies for Fading Visual Supports

A commonly asked question is whether the visual supports an individual student is using should ever be faded out completely. The short answer is: sometimes yes and sometimes no.

As stated elsewhere in this book, it is not always necessary to completely fade out supports. We all use visual supports to remind us about appointments (a calendar), tasks to be completed (a "to do" list on paper or stored on a Palm Pilot), or what we need to purchase for home (shopping list). So, using a visual support is sometimes entirely typical and appropriate.

The decision as to whether to fade or not to fade depends upon several variables:

- What do typically developing children use (e.g., a to do list, a note attached to a backpack)?
- Will the individual be able to perform as independently if the support is removed?
- What supports will members of the community readily respond to and therefore reinforce the student for using (e.g., pictures of various fast food items that can be ordered when out to lunch)?

In many cases, it is optimal to completely eliminate the support if it is not a support that a typically developing peer would use. However, if eliminating the support means that the learner is now less independent or is not understood in the general community, then continuing to use it may be the better option. Also, there are other issues to keep in mind. For instance, it's probably not a good idea to take away the support when the person is going through a stressful period such as when starting a new job or a new school, or dealing with a death or divorce. In addition, you should try to involve the person with autism in the decision to fade the support as much as possible. This may involve seeking his input about a fading strategy or talking to him about why you're making these changes and getting him to buy into them.

▨ Methods of Fading Supports

This chapter addresses several different ways in which supports can be faded. The method used must take into account the type of support created. In order to help you decide what method to use, examples are included to illustrate the fading methods best suited for each support. The list is not all-inclusive, so the reader may have to make this decision based on the examples provided. It is important to note that a support may be faded in more than one way (e.g., by size or by topography). As you get to know more about your student, you will be able to determine which method is the most effective.

Fading Supports by Size

One way to reduce or eliminate supports is to gradually make them smaller (fade the size). You can fade the size in order to make the support more portable or to remove the support entirely. When first creating the full-sized support, it is best to prepare some in smaller sizes too. That way the student can have access to a faded prompt as soon as he is ready.

One good way to fade supports by size is to use a photocopier that has a size reduction feature. Copiers with this feature are available at many office supply stores if you do not have access to your own. Depending upon your student's sensitivity to prompt fading, you can fade by as little as 10 percent or as much as 25 percent at a time.

The following visual supports shown previously in this book are good candidates for this kind of fading. An asterisk indicates that the support reappears below with an illustration of how it can be faded by size.

- Chapter 3—Figure 3.5, Social Story* (See Figure 9.1 on page 136-137)
- Chapter 4—Figure 4.4 & Figure 4.5, Photo/Word Grocery List
- Chapter 4—Figure 4.7, Color Coding (Washer)*
  (See Figure 9.2 in color insert)
- Chapter 7—Figure 7.11 & Figure 7.12, Picture Schedule

Fading Supports by Topography (Form)

A support can be faded by slowly and systematically "erasing" its form. One example is changing a solid line to a dotted line and then making the dots progressively less visible until they are no longer visible. Changing topography can be done manually (drawing each version of the visual support with increasingly faded lines, etc.) or by placing layers of wax paper (or other opaque material) over the original visual by adding one layer at a time until the form is no longer visible. Refer to Figure 9.3 on page 138 and Figure 9.4 in the color insert for an example of how this can be done. In addition, the following visual supports shown previously in this book would be good candidates for this kind of fading:

Fading Supports by Component

Sometimes a visual support such as a graphic organizer may be comprised of several parts or components. In this case, you can fade the support by eliminating one component at a time. For example, you can remove one word from a graphic organizer and require the student to fill in the blank (or missing word). Once that is accomplished, another word can be faded and so on until no words are left on the organizer. Then, each encircled offshoot on the graphic organizer can be eliminated one at a time until the page is blank.

Another example is a support for writing a name or a sight word. You can replace the last letter of the word with a blank line and have the student complete the word. Then, sequentially eliminate each additional letter until no letters are left and the student is writing the entire word without a visual support. Below are some previously illustrated visual supports that would be good candidates for this fading method.

Fading Supports When Using Multiple Components

There are several examples of visual supports that have more than one attribute (e.g., color cues and word cues for correct syntax use). For example, in the visual support shown in Figure 9.8 on page 141 (and first discussed in Chapter 3), different colored blocks are used to indicate different parts of speech, and the picture order is another support to help students understand syntax. In this case, you can begin by fading the least relevant cue first. In this example, color would be the least relevant cue because it is not directly related to syntax. This cue can be eliminated one color at a time by either selecting the first or last color in the sequence and working sequentially from that point. For example, if the color red is used to designate the subject of a complete sentence, the color blue is used to represent the verb, and the color yellow is used to represent the object, then you can remove the color red first, followed by blue, and then yellow. You could also start with eliminating the color yellow representing the object and work backwards from that point. Once the first variable (color) is eliminated, you can begin eliminating the other variable (pictures) using the same method.

Fig. 9.1

Fig. 9.3

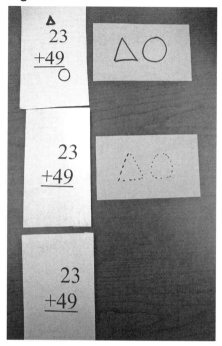

A couple of examples of visual supports shown elsewhere in the book that are good candidates for this type of fading include:

- Chapter 3—Figure 3.7, Augmenting Auditory Stimuli
- Chapter 3—Figure 3.8, Phonology
- Chapter 3—Figure 3.13, Syntax* (Figure 9.8 on page 141)
- Chapter 4—Figure 4.19, Keyboarding
- Chapter 5—Figure 5.7 & Figure 5.8, Chore Checklist* (Figure 9.9 on page 141)
- Chapter 5—Figure 5.17 & Figure 5.18, Identification of Grocery Aisle Location

Fading Supports by Trial

If you are using Discrete Trial Instruction (DTI) with a student, you can fade the visual support by eliminating it one trial at a time. For example, if you are presenting ten trials, use the visual support for the first nine trials and do not present it for the last trial. As the child becomes more independent, you can remove the support for the last two trials and so on.

It is critical to note that the skill cannot be considered mastered until *no visual support* is presented. It is possible for a student to achieve a 90 percent correct response rate and still require the support for the presentation of the first trial. In this case, the student has only demonstrated the ability to follow the prompt, rather than the ability to understand and functionally use the concept being taught.

Since this method of fading cannot be illustrated visually, the list below gives examples of the kinds of visual supports that can be faded using this method.

- Chapter 5—Figure 5.19, Addition Using Manipulatives
- Chapter 5—Figure 5.20, Organizing Place Value

Fig. 9.5

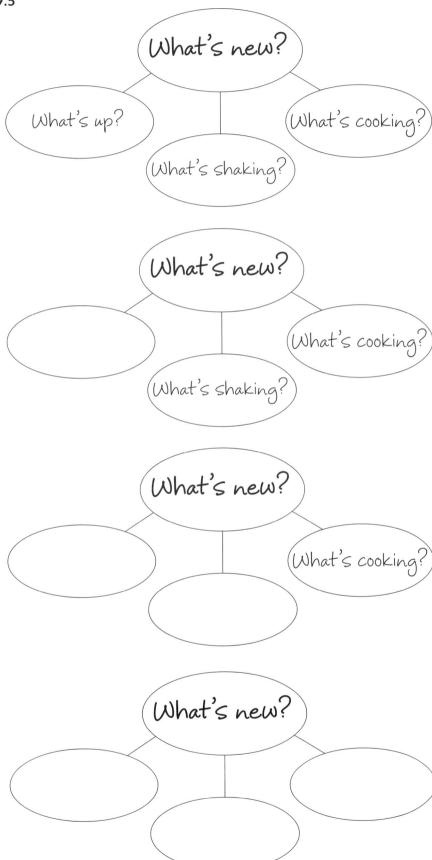

Fig. 9.6

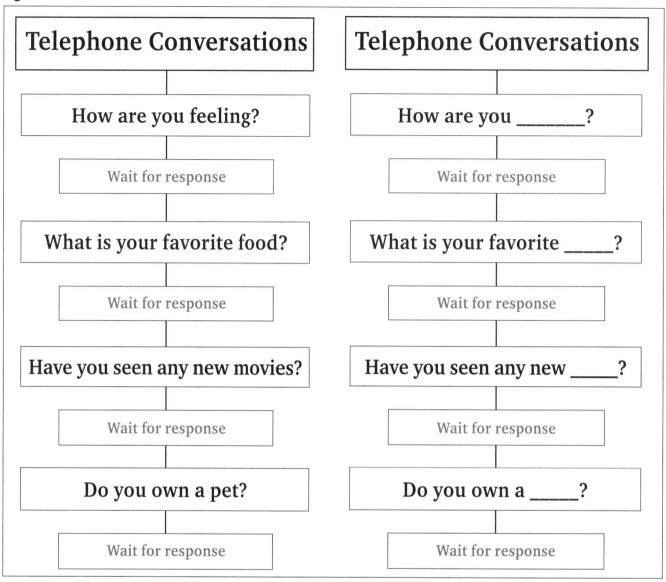

- Chapter 5—Figure 5.22, Addition/Multiplication Association
- Chapter 5—Figure 5.11, Table Setting Sequence
- Chapter 5—Figure 5.28-30, Handwriting

Fading Supports Using a Time Delay

You can also fade a visual support by introducing a time delay procedure. In this case, the first step would involve presenting the visual support immediately after the instruction. In the second step, you would wait one second before presenting the prompt, giving the student an opportunity to respond on his own. The time delay can be increased one second at a time, up to five seconds. A prompt delay that is presented more than five seconds from the instruction might serve to separate the instruction from the response and to inadvertently teach the student to respond more slowly than is optimal. The list on page 142 includes examples of the types of supports that best match this method of prompt fading.

Fig. 9.8

In the example at right, the pictures are gradually reduced in size, until only the written words are left.

Fig. 9.9

Chores	Done
1. Walk the dog	
2. Wash the dishes.	
3. Make the bed.	

Chores	Done
1. Walk the dog.	
2. Wash the dishes.	
3. Make the bed.	

Chores	Done
1. Walk the dog.	
2. Wash the dishes.	
3. Make the bed.	

- Chapter 3—Figure 3.8, Phonology
- Chapter 3—Figure 3.9, Phonology
- Chapter 3—Figure 3.13, Syntax
- Chapter 8—Figure 8.7, Starting Conversations

Fading to More Natural Appearing Supports and Schedules of Reinforcement

An important consideration to keep in mind when making decisions about fading is the generality (use in a variety of settings) of a particular visual support. You need to consider how the support fits within the natural community. In other words, does it draw negative attention to the student and is the schedule of reinforcement close to what is available in the general community?

These issues become particularly important as students become older and are expected to participate more independently within their communities. That does not mean that the support needs to be eliminated. Can you imagine going grocery shopping without a shopping list? How many items would you forget? It is common for shoppers to carry a list. Generalization to other environments is easier when a visual support is something (like a list) that is commonly used in the community.

Even if a visual support is not something that is commonly used in the community, it may be possible to make it look more natural. For example, you can make supports as small and unobtrusive as possible, make them look like something a typical child of that age would carry in public, or change from pictures to written words, if possible.

Below are examples of supports illustrated earlier in the book that are good candidates for fading to more natural schedules of reinforcement.

- Chapter 5—Figure 5.2 & Figure 5.3, Puzzle Picture Reinforcement System* (Figure 9.10)
- Chapter 7—Figure 7.11 & Figure 7.12, Task/Reinforcement Schedule* (Figure 9.11, color insert)

Fig. 9.10

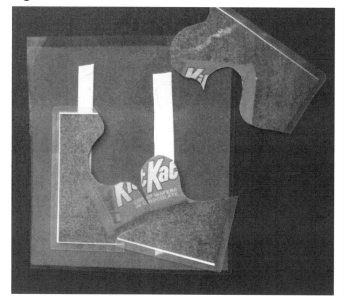 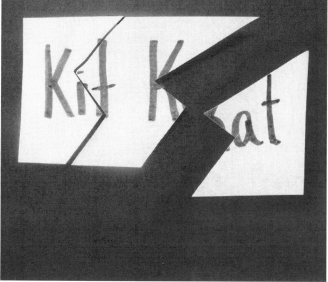

In the example shown in Figure 9.11 (color insert), a student's schedule begins as a large, wall-sized schedule. The size and form then shift to a schedule in a small binder and eventually into a wallet- or pocket-sized photo album.

Tips for Generalization

Below is a list of ideas that can be used to enhance the generalization process:

- Fade the form of a visual support to match something comparable in the community environment.
  - ❏ Chapter 5—Figure 5.9 & Figure 5.10, Hand Washing Steps— gradually switch visuals used on the support to match signs that are commonly used in the community (e.g., employee hand washing signs).
- Change the type of token used so that it matches what is used in the natural setting.
  - ❏ Chapter 7—Figure 7.3, Token System—switch from stickers or poker chips to money, which can be used to purchase a reinforcer.
  - ❏ Chapter 7—Figure 7.5, Job List Key Tokens—switch from poker chips or similar items to keys placed on a key ring.
- Incorporate functional academic skills and chain multiple skills together (for example, make a grocery list, use the list to buy items, and then use the list to check whether everything has been purchased).
  - ❏ Chapter 7—Figure 7.8, Banking System—vary the cost of reinforcement to closely match costs in the community or teach the student how to bank reinforcers and give him a choice of immediately trading them in or saving them for a reinforcer of higher value. Eventually, he can be taught to use these skills to keep a real bank account.
  - ❏ Chapter 8—Figure 8.3 (color insert), Matching Clothes—reduce reliance on pictures as supports and use words or color coding instead; switch from pictures of items that match to a color-coded system placed on the clothing tag.

Teaching Self-Monitoring

Using visual supports independently is a good goal for individuals who might be in a position to be left on their own for periods of time. Not only does this enable the child or adult with ASD to be more independent, but it also teaches responsibility and the concept of self-management.

It is best to teach the student to implement one part of the support at a time. For example, if you are teaching self-monitoring of the picture puzzle reinforcement system, you may first teach independent selection of a reinforcer. You can then teach the learner to place each piece of the puzzle on the reinforcement board. Next, you can teach him to turn the timer off, and finally, to set the timer for the correct interval.

Another example is teaching independent use of a picture or written schedule. The child can first be taught to select a single picture/word and to place it on the schedule, then complete the task/activity. Pictures/words can be added one by one until the student is able to schedule his own time for longer and longer periods. He can learn to check off each assignment as it is completed, erase it (when using a dry erase board), or to remove the picture/word and place it in a "finished" bin. The list below includes examples of the type of supports that best match this method (the method that students with ASD are most likely to learn to use independently).

- Chapter 5—Figure 5.2 & Figure 5.3, Puzzle Picture Reinforcement System
- Chapter 5—Figure 5.6, Activity Schedule
- Chapter 6—Figure 6.1 & Figure 6.2, Traffic Light to Monitor Learner Attention

■ Difficulty in Fading Visual Supports

Sometimes it is relatively easy to fade a support. Other times, the person may no longer be able to do a task when the support is faded or partially faded. Sometimes you can successfully fade one support for an individual, but not another. Difficulties in fading supports may occur because the person has become too dependent upon a specific aspect of a support (e.g., its size or its format). A good rule of thumb is to watch the person's performance. If he stops performing the skill, then you need to either troubleshoot or decide whether it is critical to fade the support.

One troubleshooting strategy is to go back to allowing the individual to use the original support and then fade the support more gradually, so it is less obvious to him that you are fading it. It can also help to provide more reinforcement for increasingly independent behavior. Even if a support cannot be faded successfully initially, try again at a later date. The child or adult with ASD may require some additional time to store the support into his memory before being asked to do the skill independently.

An Example of the Use of Visual Supports to Increase Opportunities

In the previous nine chapters, we have shared what we believe are some very effective ideas and strategies for using visual supports to help children and adults with ASD learn. What we may not have adequately expressed yet, however, is how sometimes by adding very simple modifications we can achieve big changes. We think the story of Nicholas, below, can help us illustrate the power of simple visual supports in unlocking the potential of students with autism:

Nicholas was enrolled in a public school class for students with autism in the elementary grades with several other students. At age nine, he was the oldest of the group and the teaching staff felt he was not benefiting from the present educational environment. The child study team shared the same concerns. Nicholas's mother, however, saw in him something that the educators were not seeing. She was a relentless advocate for her son and felt that, with the right modifications, he could thrive in the current classroom environment.

When I first observed Nicholas in his classroom, he engaged in frequent stereotyped behavior (noises and body movements). He did not appear to understand his picture communication system, which consisted of several pages of icons in a small binder that he was supposed to use to indicate his wants and needs. Instead, the staff would guess at what Nicholas wanted to say and prompt him to place those icons on a sentence strip and hand it to a teacher. This didn't seem to satisfy Nicholas's needs and he was not responsive to any communicative attempt during my observation. Nicholas's educational goals included many language concepts such as prepositions, body part identification, and pronoun use, but he was not making progress in learning these concepts.

The staff reported that Nicholas was not interested in interacting with the teachers or the students. He had not learned anyone's name and was having great difficulty participating in small group activities. As a result, the teaching staff were frustrated and thought that he would benefit more if he were moved to a specialized program for students with autism with a focus on more functional skill training. (In contrast, Nicholas's mother felt that he was able to learn some basic academic skills, although he was not demonstrating progress in the classroom.)

After reading this description of Nicholas, where do you think he is today? What is he doing? Three years later, Nicholas is communicating verbally with single words and short phrases. His communication is spontaneous and he uses it to engage his teachers and other students in genuine social interactions. Nicholas is succeeding in learning a variety of academic skills such as telling time using an analog clock, addition with carrying, linear measurement, and reading short stories. In addition, he is readily transferring these skills to his natural environment, often without direct instruction to do so. Nicholas also had success in inclusion experiences in a special education classroom designed for students with disabilities other than autism.

Currently, Nicholas is making a successful transition into a classroom for students with multiple disabilities in his local middle school. He is thriving in this new environment and can boast of being able to open and close his own locker. He has learned that he can do more things independently when he observes other students perform a task. This strategy allows Nicholas to take advantage of the naturally occurring visual supports in his environment.

Nicholas still requires support from an assigned 1:1 teacher in his new classroom, but he uses her support less often and is able to respond well to other instructional staff in the classroom. Although Nicholas still requires quite a bit of special educational support, he has come a long way from the days when he was completely uncommunicative and unengaged in the classroom, and his teachers wanted to transfer him to a self-contained, functional program for children with autism. For Nicholas to make the progress he has, it took three years of modifications to his educational programming involving many visual support strategies. It also required coordination and cooperation between an interdisciplinary team along with his parents to make this work. Some of the strategies used included:

- **Visual support for language:** Introduction of an augmentative computer with picture symbols that he could press on a touch screen; this was spontaneously faded to verbal communication with communication training directed at meeting his immediate needs and wants.

- **Visual support for motivation:** Incorporating a visual cue (a green go sign and a red stop sign) to indicate when he could receive reinforcement for refraining from particular stereotyped behaviors (e.g., the traffic signal was used to let him know when he was behaving appropriately, and he was subsequently rewarded for controlling his behavior).

- **Visual support for temporal/sequential skills:** A picture schedule to indicate the plans for the day and to help staff review with him any new activities or changes in the regular schedule.

■ **Visual supports for concept development/academic programs:**

❑ Flashcards with the digital time placed under an analog clock and systematically faded

❑ A Post-It© flag placed on an analog clock to indicate the slight placement difference between the hour hand when at 15 minutes before the hour and the next hour interval

❑ Written sentence strips to teach expansion of language, which were faded using a backward chain (eliminating one word at a time starting with the last word and working backwards)

❑ An organizer for double-digit addition with carrying that allowed Nicholas to place the ones place value in the ones column and move the tens value to the tens column to be carried over (see Figure 5.25)

❑ Video modeling to learn the steps of shopping in a grocery store prior to his first community experience

❑ Supportive computer software programmed by a computer consultant to reinforce spelling, reading, and social skills (e.g., IntelliTools)

❑ Digital pictures of staff with names written underneath to teach identification of people in the educational environment

These are only a few examples of the visual supports that have helped Nicholas succeed in the classroom. The important thing to remember is that this student needed additional visual cues to understand what was being taught. Once he memorized those cues, they were no longer necessary to ongoing instruction and could be faded.

We have shared Nicholas's story because the use of visual supports made a profound difference in his life. The difference opened the door to his increased independence and ability to interact successfully with peers. Some students with ASD may need more or fewer visual supports than Nicholas did. Some of the students we have worked with are successfully included in regular education classes and making good progress in the regular education curriculum, but visual supports enable them to comprehend information from the curriculum better. Other students attend school in more specialized settings where the use of visual supports enhances their learning in general (e.g., understanding when and what reinforcement will be provided).

In all of our infinite wisdom, we cannot truly know the capabilities of our students. If we give up because we have exhausted our current strategies, we will shortchange our learners in reaching their ultimate goals. We have good news! It is never too late. Many older children and adults with autism have benefited tremendously from the introduction of visual support strategies. Use our examples. Create your own. See what works best for each individual student. The outcome is well worth the effort.

References

 Chapter 1

Bainbridge, N. & Myles, B.S. (1999). The use of priming to introduce toilet training to a child with autism. *Focus on Autism and Other Developmental Disabilities, 14(2)*, 106-109.

Holland, S. (2002). Traditional color deficiency tests. Hidden Talents website (http://members.shaw.ca/hidden-talents/vision/color/colorblind2.html).

MacDuff, G.S., Krantz, P.J. & McClannahan, L.E. (1993). Teaching children with autism to use photographic activity schedules: Maintenance and generalization of complex response chains. *Journal of Applied Behavior Analysis 26,* 89-97.

Pierce, K.C. & Schreibamn, L. (1994). Teaching daily living skills to children with autism in unsupervised settings through pictorial self-management. *Journal of Applied Behavior Analysis 27,* 471-481.

 Chapter 2

Baker, J.E. (2003). *The Social Skills Picture Book: Teaching Play, Emotion, and Communication to Children with Autism.* Arlington, TX: Future Horizons.

Baker, J.E. (2003). *Social Skills Training for Children and Adolescents with Asperger Syndrome and Social-Communication Problems.* Shawnee Mission, KS: Autism Asperger Publishing Company.

Bondy, A. & Frost, L. (2002). *A Picture's Worth: PECS and Other Visual Communication Strategies in Autism.* Bethesda, MD: Woodbine House.

Bromley, K., Irwin-DeVitis, L. & Modlo, M. (1995). *Graphic Organizers: Visual Strategies for Active Learning.* New York, NY: Scholastic.

Charlop-Christy, M.H., LeLoc, M. & Freeman, K.A. (2000). A comparison of video modeling with in-vivo modeling for teaching children with autism. *Journal of Autism and Developmental Disorders 30,* 532-537.

Corbett, B.A. (2003). Video modeling applications for children with autism spectrum disorders. Presentation conducted at the M.I.N.D. Institute, Department of Psychiatry and Behavioral Sciences.

Gagnon, E. (2001). *Power Cards.* Shawnee Mission, KS: Autism Asperger Publishing Co.

Glaeser, B.C., Pierson, M.R. & Fritschamnn, N. (2003). Comic strip conversations: A positive behavioral support strategy. *Teaching Exceptional Children 36(2),* 14-19.

Gray, C. (1994). *Comic Strip Conversations.* Arlington, TX: Future Horizons.

Gray, C. (1995). *Social Stories Unlimited: Social Stories and Comic Strip Conversations.* Jenison, MI: Jenison Public Schools.

Haring, T., Kennedy, C., Adams, M. & Pitts-Conway, V. (1987). Teaching generalization of purchasing skills across community settings to autistic youth using videotape modeling. *Journal of Applied Behavior Analysis 20,* 89-96.

Jacobson, J. & Raymer, D. (1999). *The Big Book of Reproducible Graphic Organizers.* New York, NY: Scholastic Professional Books.

Kuttler, S., Myles, B.S. & Carlson, J.K. (1998). The use of social stories to reduce precursors of tantrum behavior in a student with autism. *Focus on Autism and Other Developmental Disabilities 13(3),* 176-182.

McClannahan, L.E. & Krantz, P.J. (1999). *Activity Schedules for Children with Autism: Teaching Independent Behavior.* Bethesda, MD: Woodbine House.

Regional School District 15, Middlebury and Southbury, Connecticut. Region 15 graphic organizers. (http://www.region15.org/curriculum/graphicorg.html).

Vaugh, B. & Horner, H. (1995). Effects of concrete versus verbal choice systems on problem behavior. *Augmentative and Alternative Communication 11,* 89-92.

Voss, K. S. *Teaching by Design: Using Your Computer to Create Materials for Students with Learning Differences.* Bethesda, MD: Woodbine House, 2005.

■ Chapter 3

Frith, U. (1989). *Autism: Explaining the Enigma*. Cambridge, MA: Blackwell Publishers.

Gagnon, E. (2001). *Power Cards*. Shawnee Mission, KS: Autism Asperger Publishing Co.

Gallaudet University (1983). *The Comprehensive Signed English Dictionary*. Washington, DC.: Gallaudet University Press.

The Graphic Organizer. www.graphic.org.

Gray, C. (1994). *Comic Strip Conversations*. Arlington, TX: Future Horizons.

Gray, C. (1995). *Social Stories Unlimited: Social Stories and Comic Strip Conversations*. Jenison, MI: Jenison Public Schools.

Levine, M. (1994). *Educational Care: A System for Understanding and Helping Children with Learning Problems at Home and in School*. Cambridge, MA: Educators Publishing Service, Inc.

Phelps-Terasaki, D. & Phelps-Gunn, T. (1989). *Syntax-Flip-Book*. Austin, TX: ProEd.

■ Chapter 4

Cooper, J.O., Heron. T.E. & Heward, W.L. (1987). *Applied Behavior Analysis*. Englewood Cliffs, NJ: Prentice Hall.

EdHelper.com. Graphic organizers. http://www.edHelper.com/teachers/graphic_organizers.html

Gagnon, E. (2001). *Power Cards*. Shawnee Mission, KS: Autism Asperger Publishing.

Hallahan, D.P. & Kauffman, J.M. (2000). *Exceptional Learners: Introduction to Special Education*. 8th ed. Needham Heights, MA: Pearson Education Company.

Lerner, J. (2003). *Learning Disabilities: Theories, Diagnosis, and Teaching Strategies*. New York, NY: Houghton Mifflin Co.

Levine, M. (1994). *Educational Care: A System for Understanding and Helping Children with Learning Problems at Home and in School*. Cambridge, MA: Educators Publishing Service.

McClannahan, L.E. & Krantz, P.J. (1999). *Activity Schedules for Children with Autism: Teaching Independent Behavior*. Bethesda, Maryland: Woodbine House.

Parish, P. (1991). *Adventures of Amelia Bedelia*. New York: Harper Collins.

Sousa, D.A. (2001). *How the Special Needs Brain Learns*. Thousand Oaks, CA: Corwin Press.

Chapter 5

Gagnon, E. (2001). *Power Cards*. Shawnee Mission, KS: Asperger Publishing Co.

Gardom, T. & Milner, A. (1993). *The Natural History Museum Book of Dinosaurs*. London: Carlton Books Limited.

Lerner, J. (2003). *Learning Disabilities: Theories, Diagnosis, and Teaching Strategies*. New York, NY: Houghton Mifflin.

Levine, M. (1994). *Educational Care: A System for Understanding and Helping Children with Learning Problems at Home and in School*. Cambridge, MA: Educators Publishing Service.

Marnell, L. J. (2001). *Creative Cursive Handbook* and *Learn Letters Workbook*. Available from Therapro (225 Arlington St., Framingham, MA 01702; www. theraproducts.com).

McClannahan, L.E. & Krantz, P.J. (1999). *Activity Schedules for Children with Autism: Teaching Independent Behavior*. Bethesda, MD: Woodbine House.

Chapter 6

Cooper, J. O., Heron, T.E. & Heward, H.L. (1987). *Applied Behavior Analysis*. Upper Saddle River, NJ: Prentice Hall.

Gagnon, E. (2001). *Power Cards*. Shawnee Mission, KS: Autism Asperger Publishing Co.

Levine, M. (1994). *Educational Care: A System for Understanding and Helping Children with Learning Problems at Home and in School*. Cambridge, MA: Educators Publishing Service.

Pike, R.W. (1989). *Creative Training Techniques Handbook*. Minneapolis, MN: Lakewood Books.

Sousa, D.A. (2001). *How the Special Needs Brain Learns*. Thousand Oaks, CA: Corwin Press.

Chapter 7

Delmolino, L. & Harris, S.L. (2004). *Incentives for Change: Motivating People with Autism Spectrum Disorders to Learn and Gain Independence.* Bethesda, MD: Woodbine House.

Gagnon, E. (2001) *Power Cards.* Shawnee Mission, KS: Autism Asperger Publishing Co.

Gray, C. (1995). *Social Stories Unlimited: Social Stories and Comic Strip Conversations.* Jenison, MI: Jenison Public Schools.

Levine, M. (1994). *Educational Care: A System for Understanding and Helping Children with Learning Problems at Home and in School.* Cambridge, MA: Educators Publishing Service.

Chapter 8

Bacon, A., Fein, D., Morris, R., Waterhouse, L. & Allen, D. (1998). Responses of autistic children to the distress of others. *Journal of Autism and Developmental Disorders 28,* 129-142.

Baker, J. E. (2003). *The Social Skills Picture Book.* Arlington, TX: Future Horizons.

Frith, U. (1989). *Autism: Explaining the Enigma.* Cambridge, MA: Blackwell Publishers.

Gagnon, E. (2001). *Power Cards.* Shawnee Mission, KS: Autism Asperger Publishing Co.

Gray, C. (1995). *Social Stories Unlimited: Social Stories and Comic Strip Conversations.* Jenison, MI: Jenison Public Schools.

Levine, M. (1994). *Educational Care: A System for Understanding and Helping Children with Learning Problems at Home and in School.* Cambridge, MA: Educators Publishing Service.

McClannahan, L.E. & Krantz, P.J. (1999). *Activity Schedules for Children with Autism.* Bethesda, MD: Woodbine House.

▇ Recommended Reading

Baker, J.E. (2003). *Social Skills Training for Children and Adolescents with Asperger Syndrome and Social-Communication Problems.* Shawnee Mission, KS: Autism Asperger Publishing Co.

Bondy, A. & Frost, L. (2001). *A Picture's Worth: PECS and Other Visual Communication Strategies in Autism.* Bethesda, MD: Woodbine House.

Cooper, J.O., Heron. T.E. & Heward, W.L. (1987). *Applied Behavior Analysis.* Upper Saddle River, NJ: Prentice Hall.

Delmolino, L. & Harris, S.L. (2004). *Incentives for Change: Motivating People with Autism Spectrum Disorders to Learn and Gain Independence.* Bethesda, MD: Woodbine House.

Gagnon, E. (2001) *Power Cards.* Shawnee Mission, KS: Autism Asperger Publishing Co.

Gray, C. (1994). *Comic Strip Conversations.* Arlington, TX: Future Horizons.

Gray, C. (2000). *The New Social Story Book.* Arlington, TX: Future Horizons.

Hodgdon, L. (1995). *Visual Strategies for Improving Communication: Practical Supports for School and Home.* Troy, MI: Quirk Roberts. [Also available in Spanish.]

Horstmeier, D. (2004). *Teaching Math to People with Down Syndrome and Other Hands-on Learners.* Bethesda, MD: Woodbine House.

Levine, M. (2002). *A Mind at a Time.* New York, NY: Simon & Schuster.

Levine, M. (2003). *The Myth of Laziness.* New York, NY: Simon & Schuster.

McClannahan, L.E. & Krantz, P.J. (1999). *Activity Schedules: Teaching Independent Behavior.* Bethesda, MD: Woodbine House.

Novak, J.D., Gowin, D.B. & Kahle, J.B. (1984). *Learning How to Learn.* Cambridge, UK: Cambridge University Press.

Pike, R.W. (1989). *Creative Training Techniques Handbook.* Minneapolis, MN: Lakewood Books.

Powers, M.D. (2000). *Children with Autism: A Parents' Guide (2nd edition).* Bethesda, MD: Woodbine House.

Smith Myles, B. & Simpson, R.L. (1998). *Asperger Syndrome: A Guide for Educators and Parents.* Austin, TX: Pro-Ed.

Sousa, D.A. (2001). *How the Special Needs Brain Learns.* Thousand Oaks, CA: Corwin Press.

Voss, K.S. (2005). *Teaching by Design: Using Your Computer to Create Materials for Students with Learning Differences.* Bethesda, MD: Woodbine House.

Weiss, M.J. & Harris, S.L. (2001). *Reaching Out, Joining In: Teaching Social Skills to Young Children with Autism.* Bethesda, MD: Woodbine House.

Resource Guide

◼ National Organizations

ASPEN of America (Asperger Syndrome Education Network of America)
P.O. Box 2577
Jacksonville, FL 32203-2577
904-745-6741
www.asperger.org
　　A national organization that provides information about Asperger's Syndrome to parents and professionals.

Autism Society of America
7910 Woodmont Avenue, Suite 300
Bethesda, MD 20814
800-3-AUTISM; 301-657-0881
www.autism-society.org
　　A national organization of parents and professionals that promotes a better understanding of autism, encourages the development of services, supports research related to autism and advocates on behalf of people with autism and their families. Acts as an information clearinghouse about autism and services for people with autism. Publishes the *Advocate,* a bimonthly newsletter. Coordinates a national network of affiliated state and local chapters.

Center for the Study of Autism
P.O. Box 4538
Salem, OR 97302
www.autism.org
　　Conducts research into therapies and provides information to parents through its website. Affiliated with the Autism Research Institute.

The Doug Flutie, Jr. Foundation for Autism
c/o The Giving Back Fund
54 Canal Street, Suite 320
Boston, MA 02114
617-556-2820
www.dougflutiejrfoundation.org
    This nonprofit foundation provides funding for services for economically disadvantaged families and for research into the causes and treatment of autism. It also serves as a clearinghouse of information about innovative programs and services for children with autism.

The Indiana Resource Center for Autism
Institute for the Study of Developmental Disabilities
Indiana University
2853 East Tenth Street
Bloomington, IN 47408-2601
812-855-6508; 812-855-9396 (TTY)
www.iidc.indiana.edu/~irca
    Conducts outreach training and consultations, engages in research, and develops and disseminates information focused on building the capacity of local communities, organizations, and families to support children and adults across the autism spectrum in typical work, school, home, and community settings.

Learning Disabilities Association of America (LDA)
4156 Library Road
Pittsburgh, PA 15234-1349
412-341-1515
www.ldanatl.org
    With over 500 local affiliates, this national organization supports people with learning disabilities and their families. It publishes a wide variety of information about the many different learning disabilities, and can provide information on educational programs, laws, and advocacy.

National Dissemination Center for Children with Disabilities (NICHCY)
P.O. Box 1492
Washington, DC 20013
800-695-0285; 202-884-8200 (voice/TDD)
www.nichcy.org
    An invaluable organization that links parents to practically every government and nonprofit agency and organization involved in any way with disabilities. NICHCY's website provides extensive links and resources, organized into "State Resource Sheet."

New Jersey Center for Outreach & Services for the Autism Community (COSAC)
1450 Parkside Avenue, Suite 22
Ewing, NJ 08638
609-883-8100; 800-4-AUTISM (in NJ)
www.njcosac.org
  An organization that provides parent support, information referral, advocacy on behalf of people with autism and related conditions, and provides community support services. Its National Directory of programs and services for the autism community is extremely useful.

Nonverbal Learning Disabilities Association (NLDA)
2446 Albany Ave
West Hartford, CT 06117
860-570-0217
www.nlda.org
  Children with NLD tend to have good verbal abilities, but difficulties with nonverbal tasks, such as visual-spatial skills, math, and organization. NLD is common in children with Asperger syndrome. The NLDA, a membership organization, offers an online forum, informational articles, and conferences.

 # Internet Resources
Asperger's Disorder

Asperger's Disorder Homepage
www.aspergers.com
  Provides information about Asperger's disorder, along with resource listings.

Online Asperger Syndrome Information & Support (OASIS)
www.udel.edu/bkirby/asperger
  A useful website containing a wide variety of information and resources on Asperger's disorder.

Autism

Autism and PDD Support Network
www.autism-pdd.net
  A massive collection of autism-related resources, information, and links.

Autism Resources
www.autism-resources.com
  Perhaps the most comprehensive collection of useful links on autism and related topics available online.

Disabilities in General

Family Village
www.familyvillage.wisc.edu/index.html
 Online articles about specific disabilities and medical, legal, and educational issues; links; online forums.

NICHCY
www.nichcy.org
 Articles and fact sheets about specific disabilities, as well as topics of general interest such as special education and positive behavioral supports.

Graphic Organizers

The Graphic Organizer
www.graphic.org
 Great resource for creating and using graphic organizers; has many useful links and articles.

Houghton Mifflin Education Place
www.eduplace.com/graphicorganizer
 This publisher has posted a variety of graphic organizers, in English and Spanish, that are copyrighted but available for use in classrooms.

Mrs. Mitchell's Virtual School: Graphic Organizers
www.kathimitchell.com/graphorg.htm
 Links to many sites that offer free graphic organizers, including some in Spanish.

Scholastic
www.scholastic.com
 By searching for "graphic organizers" on this publisher's website, you can find a variety of graphic organizers excerpted from their publications, as well as view a number of books that contain graphic organizers.

TeacherVision.com
www.teachervision.com
 This website offers, by subscription, access to many graphic organizers, lesson plans, and ideas for teachers.

Pictures/Photographs

 Here is just a small sampling of the many websites where photographs or clipart can be downloaded for free.

AllFreeClipart.com
www.allfreeclipArt.com

Classroom Clipart
www.classroomclipart.com

DiscoverySchool.com: Clipart
http://school.discovery.com/clipart/index.html

FreeFoto.com
www.freefoto.com

Free Stock Photos
www.freestockphotos.com

Microsoft Office Clipart and Media Home Page
http://office.microsoft.com/clipart

School-Clip-Art.com—Educational Clipart
www.school-clip-art.com

Smithsonian Images
www.smithsonianimages.com

United States Department of Agriculture On Line Photography Center
www.usda.gov/oc/photo/opclibra.htm

United States Government Graphics and Photos
www.firstgov.gov/Topics/Graphics/shtml

Other Useful Sites

Americans with Disabilities Act Document Center
www.jan.wvu.edu/links/adalinks.htm
Provides online copies of ADA Statute, regulations, ADAAG (Americans with
Disabilities Act Accessibility Guidelines), federally reviewed tech sheets, and
other assistance documents.

Semantic Pragmatic Disorder Support
www.spdsupport.org.uk/socialstories.html
The website includes a section with guidance in writing Social Stories and Comic
Strip Conversations as well as devising visual timetables (schedules)

Social Skills Training Project
www.socialskillstrainingproject.com

Study Guides and Strategies
www.studygs.net

Products

Different Roads to Learning
12 West 18th St., Suite 3E
New York, NY 10011
800-853-1057; 212-604-9637
info@difflearn.com
www.difflearn.com
    A source of materials useful for teaching children with autism spectrum disorders, including many visual supports and a visual timer.

Gander Publishing
412 Higuera St., Suite 200
San Luis Obispo, CA 93401
800-554-1819
customerservice@ganderpublishing.com
www.ganderpublishing.com
    This company sells products by the Lindamood Bell Company designed to help children with learning disabilities and other learning problems master math and reading skills, as well as picture cards and other learning materials.

The Gray Center for Social Learning and Understanding
4123 Embassy Dr., SE
Kentwood, MI 49546
616-954-9749
www.thegraycenter.org/socialstories.cfm
    The official source for books, videos, DVDs, and training on how to write Social Stories™.

Great Ideas for Teaching
P.O. Box 444
Wrightsville Beach, NC 28480-0444
800-839-8339; 910-256-4494
www.greatideasforteaching.com
    Materials for speech and language learning, including picture cards, software, games.

Innovative Learning Concepts
6760 Corporate Dr.
Colorado Springs, CO 80919
800-888-9191
www.touchmath.com
    Makers of the TouchMath series of teaching products.

Inspiration Software
9400 SW Beaverton-Hillsdale Hwy., Suite 300
Beaverton, OR 97005
800-877-4292
customerservice@inspiration.com
www.inspiration.com
　　　Software tools such as Inspiration and Kidspiration to help with organization and planning.

Learning Resources
380 N. Fairway Dr.
Vernon Hills, IL 60061
800-222-3909
www.learningresources.com
　　　Offers a wide range of instructional materials, including many manipulatives and games and the Time Tracker™.

Mayer-Johnson LLC
P.O. Box 1579
Solana Beach, CA 92075
858-550-0084; 858-550-0449 (fax)
mayerj@mayer-johnson.com
www.mayer-johnson.com
　　　Mayer-Johnson is the creator of the Picture Communication Symbols (PCS), which are available in digital format through their various Boardmaker™ software programs.

Pyramid Educational Products
5-C Garfield Way
Newark, DE 19713
www.pyramidproducts.com
　　　Products designed for teachers and parents who use PECS (the Picture Exchange Communication System).

Silver Lining Multimedia
P.O. Box 544
Peterborough, NH 03458
888-777-0875
info@silverliningmm.com
www.silverliningmm.com
　　　Specializes in software with full color photographic images; also sells materials for making communication boards, photo schedules, and other visual supports; timers; videos/DVDs.

Super Duper, Inc.
P.O. Box 24997
Greenville, SC
29616-2497
800-277-8737
custserv@superduperinc.com
www.superduperinc.com
    Educational materials, including many geared specifically for teaching children with autism.

Zoo-phonics
20950 Ferretti Rd.
Groveland, CA 95321
800-622-8104; 209-962-5030
zoo-info@zoo-phonics.com
www.zoo-phonics.com

Index

About the Authors

Marlene J. Cohen is the Director of Adult and Transitional Services at the Douglass Developmental Disabilities Center and a part-time lecturer for the Graduate School of Education, both located at Rutgers University.

Donna L. Sloan is the Assistant Director of Adult and Transitional Services at the Douglass Developmental Disabilities Center. They are both Board Certified Behavior Analysts, working with adolescents and adults on the autism spectrum. Dr. Cohen and Ms. Sloan live in central New Jersey.

Fig. 3.13

Fig. 3.14

The girl is throwing the ball.

Fig. 3.15

The boy is baking brownies in the kitchen.

Fig. 3.19

Fig. 4.8

Cold water

warm water

Fig. 4.9

Type of Stuff	Water Temp— wash/rinse cycle
Whites (underwear, socks)	Hot/Cold
Light Colors (shirts)	Warm/Cold
Dark Colors (jeans)	Warm/Cold
Delicates (sweaters, knits, velour)	Cold/Cold

Fig. 4.19

Fig. 4.20

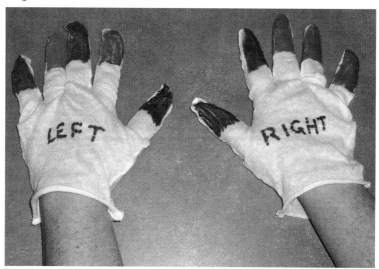

Fig. 5.1a

Fig. 5.1b

Fig. 5.1c

Fig. 5.13

1st Period: ENGLISH

Fig. 5.14

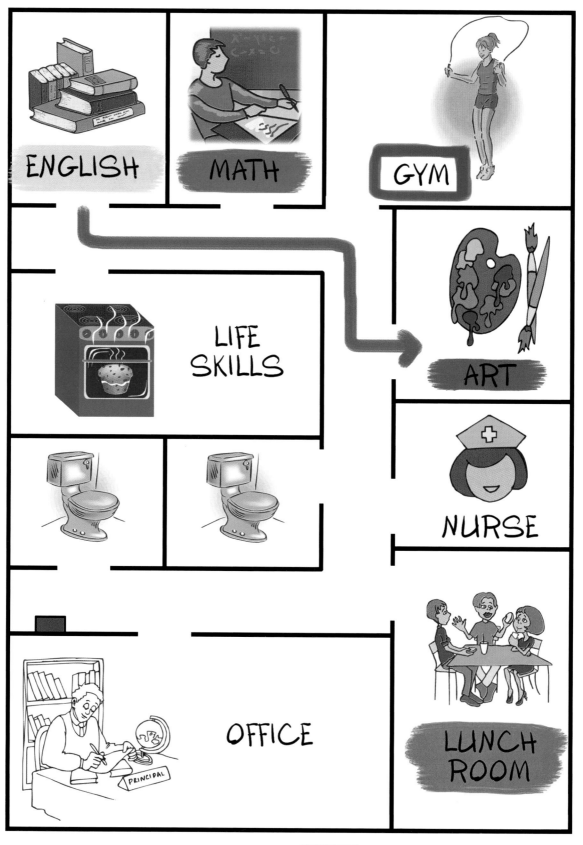

2nd Period: ART

Fig. 5.15

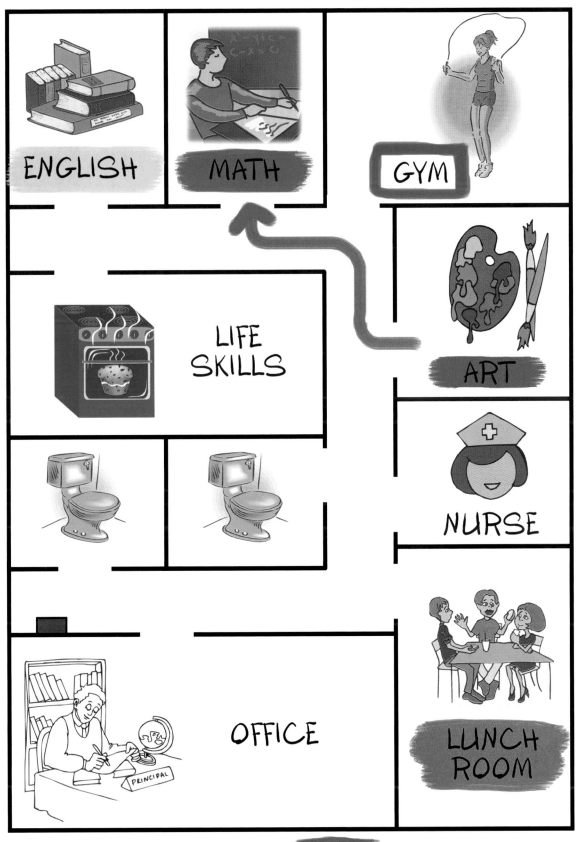

3rd Period: MATH

Fig. 5.16

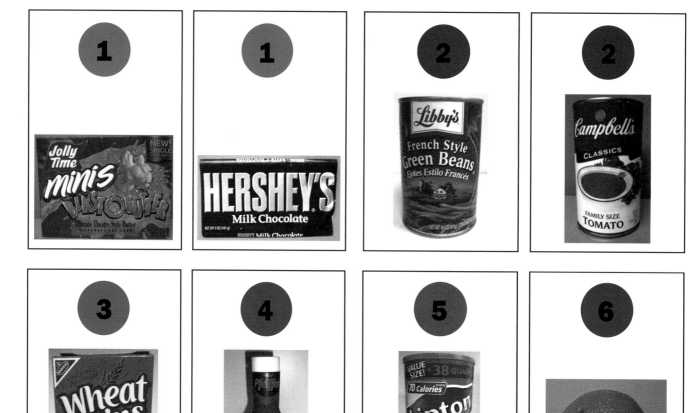

Fig. 5.17

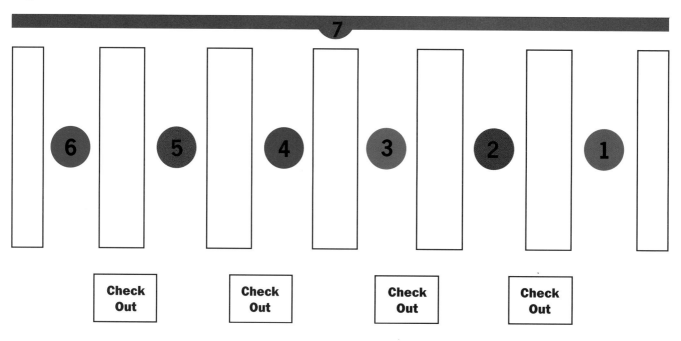

Fig. 6.1

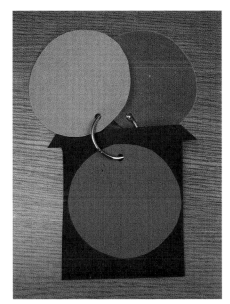

Fig. 6.2

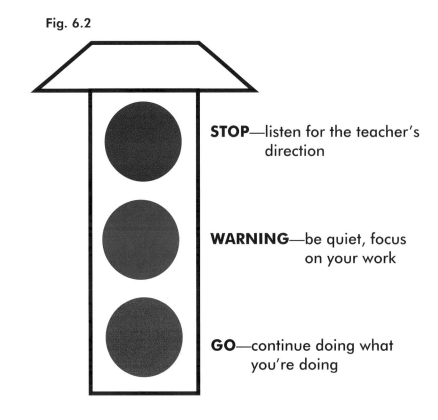

STOP—listen for the teacher's direction

WARNING—be quiet, focus on your work

GO—continue doing what you're doing

Fig. 6.8

$$6 \times 4 =$$

$$8 + 7 =$$

$$15 - 6 =$$

$$24 \div 3 =$$

Fig.7.12

Daily Schedule	Finished
1. Collect trash from offices	
2. Vacuum offices	
3. Sweep hallway	
4. Dust hallway	
5. Refill toilet paper holders	
6. BREAK TIME in Café	
7. Clean toilets	
8. Clean sinks and mirrors	
9. Collect trash from bathroom	
10. Sweep bathroom floors	
11. Mop bathroom floors	
12. LUNCH at Wendy's	
13. Collect trash outside	
14. Sweep sidewalks	
15. Wash windows	
16. BREAK in computer room	
17. Distribute mail	
18. Make photo copies	
19. Craft activity	
20. AWP – Bowling Alley	

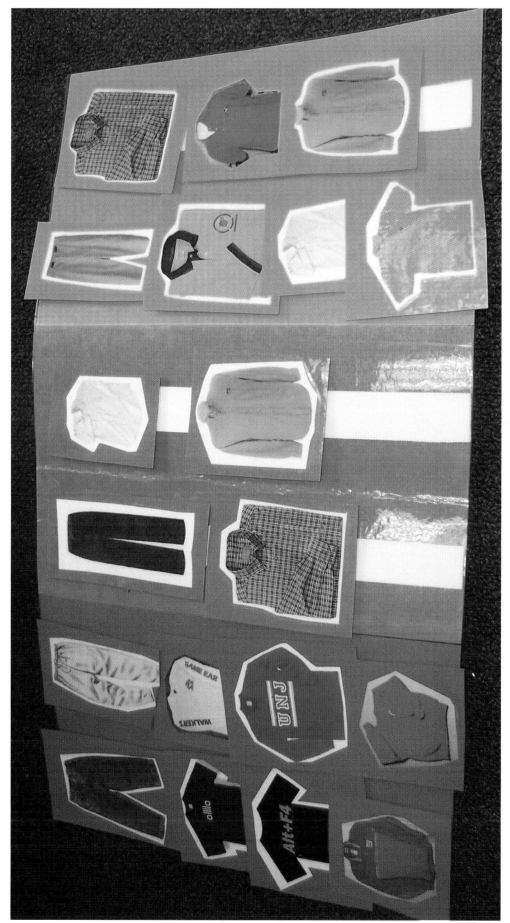

Fig. 8.3

Fig.8.13

Fig.9.2

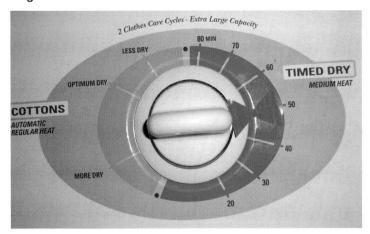

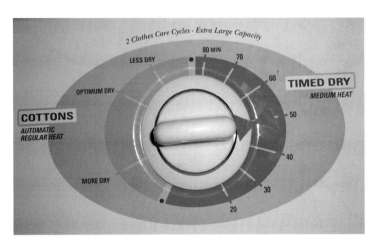

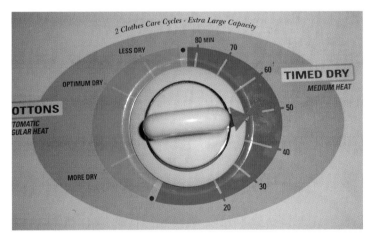

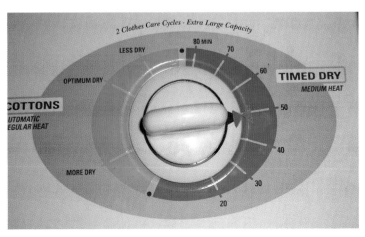